# African Arts: Contemporary Forms

CW00432108

...art Murray

EDITORIAL BOARD
Fiona Becket
Sam Durrant
Lynette Hunter
John McLeod
Neil Murphy
Brendon Nicholls
Jane Plastow
Wai-chew Sim

ADVISORY BOARD
Martin Banham
Catherine Batt
Elleke Boehmer
Susan Burns
Denise deCaires Narain
Romesh Gunesekera
Githa Hariharan
Salima Hashmi
Elaine Ho
Koh Tai Ann
Bénédicte Ledent
Russell McDougall
Niyi Osundare
Nima Poovaya-Smith
David Richards
Bede Scott
Aritha van Herk
Mark Williams

PRODUCTION
Glenda Pattenden

EDITORIAL ASSISTANT
Michelle Chiang

VOLUME 14 NUMBER 1 2014

*Moving Worlds* is a biannual international magazine. It publishes creative, critical, literary, and visual texts. Contributions of unpublished material are invited. Books for notice are welcome. Manuscripts should be double-spaced with footnotes gathered at the end, and should conform to the MHRA (Modern Humanities Research Association) Style Sheet. Wherever possible the submission should be on disc (soft-ware preferably Word for Windows, Wordperfect or Macwrite saved for PC on PC formatted disc) and should be accompanied by a hard copy. Please include a short biography, address, and email contact if available.

*Moving Worlds* is an internationally refereed journal based at the University of Leeds. The editors do not necessarily endorse the views expressed by its contributors.

All correspondence – manuscripts, books for review, enquiries – should be sent to: The Editor, *Moving Worlds*, School of English, University of Leeds, Leeds LS2 9JT, UK

email: mworlds@leeds.ac.uk
http://www.movingworlds.net

SUBSCRIPTION RATES FOR 2014
Individuals: 1 year £32.00 includes postage
Institutions: 1 year £62.00 includes postage
Students: 1 year £14.00 includes postage
Cheques should be made payable to: University of Leeds (Moving Worlds)
Payment is accepted by Visa or Mastercard, please contact Moving Worlds for details

Published by *Moving Worlds*
at School of English
University of Leeds
Leeds UK
LS2 9JT

with Division of English
Nanyang Technological University
Singapore 637332

ISBN 978-0-9567889-6-2                    ISSN 1474-4600

Printed and bound in Great Britain by
Marston Book Services Limited, Oxfordshire

# Contents

# Acknowledgements

*Moving Worlds* is published with funding assistance from the School of English, University of Leeds. UK, and School of Humanities and Social Sciences, NTU, Singapore. This issue is part funded by a contribution from the Department of English, University of Edinburgh.

We would like to thank all the contributors to this journal.

Cover photos
Front: 'Ori' in Vienna © Courtesy Adedayo Liadi 2008
Back: Female figurines framed composition, shot on the Gorè island of Dakar, Senegal © Waddle/iStockphoto 2005

# Nelson Rohihlahla Mandela: A Tribute

## ELLEKE BOEHMER

There was something about the ordinariness of Nelson Mandela, the down-to-earth, understated everydayness of the man, even when weighed alongside his many larger-than-life heroic qualities, that was perhaps one of his most inspiring features. It is a feature that stands out very prominently now, in the still palpable aftermath of his death, on 6 December 2013. This is so despite the amount that has already been said, understandably, about his greatness and goodness, his charisma and aura as a leader, his brilliance in persuading his movement to follow the path of reconciliation in race-riven 1990s South Africa, his canniness in facing down his opposition, both that of his apartheid era enemies, and the resistance mounted by those within his own party who disagreed on how to sue for peace.

Yet the word *ordinariness* such as I use it here does not merely designate 'the common touch', though Mandela was able to project that persuasively when he desired. He also routinely assured not only the very famous but also the relatively unknown that meeting them represented the best day of his life. The word also does not refer to Mandela's repeated efforts, whenever discussions of the achievement of democracy in South Africa arose in his hearing, to deflect attention away from his own individual contribution and lay emphasis on being 'only one in a large army of people', as he explained to Oprah Winfrey. By *ordinariness* I rather mean Mandela's astonishing ability to persuade his interlocutor, whether political friend or foe, that their hopes and expectations were no different from his, that is, were low-key, modest, sensible, and yet at the same time special, valid, and humanly achievable; his ability, in other words, to establish common ground with that interlocutor, yet persuade them that this was elevated ground, because they were walking it alongside Mandela himself. I am referring therefore to an out-of-the-ordinary ordinariness, that uncommon common touch upon which Mandela's entire political success rested, as did his other, equally remarkable, achievement, which is captured in the concept *African humanism*. The African humanism Mandela espoused rested on the understanding that the African far from being other or different – as racism would have it – could in fact be regarded as definitively human: human to the core. These two approaches, ordinariness and humanism, will I believe be counted as forming a central part of Mandela's legacy, alongside of course his incredible courage and resilience, and his strength of character in surviving 27.5 years of incarceration.

Both as a young politician and activist in the 1950s, and then later, as an elder statesman and South Africa's first democratic president, Mandela worked to channel his innate qualities of personal charm and self-discipline into becoming a source of inspiration and hope for his people, and did so by convincing them that these qualities might be equally achievable in their lives – another definition of the ordinariness I am trying to capture. Mandela in other words was as humanly complicated as the next man, yet was happy to convince all comers that to be so was perfectly all right, including for a political leader. This ability to appeal to the other as the self is often reflected in his speeches, which were otherwise distinguished by their lack of distinction, the woodenness of the delivery, and their over-reliance on cliché, or a few set-piece Manichean motifs (wrong v. right, white injustice v. black justice). Mandela's rhetoric tended to be language from which affect and complexity had been extracted. His clichés therefore offered a highly effective way of establishing concord and agreement with his listeners – as opposed to alienating them with high-flown language.

Nelson Mandela was above all a man of concord. When he observed that friend and foe in South Africa by and large shared the same aims, fears and desires, he forged reciprocity where none had hoped to find it. He took the hands of his gaoler and his comrade, and joined them together by pointing out that at the end of the day it was the same piece of earth that they were fighting for. Where previously there had been division and hate, he forged interaction. He deserves to be remembered therefore not simply as an icon, but as a towering figure of ordinary humanness and immense courage. He is, as the poet Jeremy Cronin puts it, an undoubted symbol of freedom but one with hands that were 'pudgy' and humanly reassuring. His spirit will live on because of the extraordinary human being he was and the superhuman sacrifices he made.

# Editorial

## JANE PLASTOW

This issue of *Moving Worlds* celebrates the range of literary and performing arts being made across Africa today. The idea for the volume came out of the African Studies Association conference hosted by Leeds University Centre for African Studies in 2012, and our focus on Ngũgĩ results from papers given at the event. East Africa's leading writer, Ngũgĩ wa Thiong'o, was the keynote speaker and his lecture is reproduced here. Ngũgĩ's impassioned call for the promotion of African language literatures is followed by two articles from Leeds scholars engaging with aspects of his work. My own article focuses on how working with ordinary Kenyans in the process of making theatre in the late 1970s had a profound impact on Ngũgĩ, and led to his commitment to cultural production in local languages. The article also touches on the novel, *Petals of Blood,* which is the subject of Brendon Nicholls' contribution, where he reads the text as concerned with imperial, generational, and gendered understandings of history.

As well as drawing on a number of papers from the African Studies conference, I have commissioned work from scholars and artists I know to be working on diverse cultural forms across a wide range of African nations. It is a particular privilege to publish creative works by authors who are household names in their own countries, but little known in the Anglophone world. Alemseged Tesfai is a novelist, playwright, and historian, usually writing in Tigrinya. He was part of Eritrea's liberation struggle, living as a freedom fighter throughout the 1970s and 1980s. His short story, *The Day Weki Burned,* is based in fact and tells of an episode in his life as a fighter that reveals, with tenderness and wit, much about the ideology and human relationships of those who won the Eritrean liberation war. Mário Lúcio Sousa is renowned in the Lusophone world as a musician, but Cape Verde knows him also as a novelist, poet, painter and playwright, and as first, minister, and now, ambassador, for culture. I was delighted when I was approached by Christina McMahon and Eunice Ferreira with the proposal that we publish a translation they undertook from Portuguese into English of Sousa's one-woman play, *Alone Onstage.* We also profile three poets whose work shows something of the range of form and theme in contemporary African poetry. Susan Kiguli and Mildred Barya are Ugandan women whose work has been garnering critical acclaim internationally in recent years, while Okinba Launko is the name the renowned Nigerian playwright, Femi Osofisan, uses for his poetry.

The other articles in this volume deal with oral poetry and music in South Africa and Uganda (Kiguli), Cape Verdean theatre (McMahon), rap music in Rwanda (Grant) and Nigerian contemporary dance (Okoye). Each focuses on particular performers and performance companies, but collectively they raise a range of issues about how contemporary arts are developing and regarded in their home settings. At one end of the spectrum Kiguli's article on oral poets and musicians compellingly discusses how many see themselves as divinely inspired – even instructed – and how they view external influences of book learning or international travel as actively harmful to their creative voices. At the same time, she touches on the tendency of African academics to make light of these claims and see the claimants as charlatans. Okoye examines the objections raised by certain African cultural critics that contemporary dance as an art form is not 'authentic'. As Okoye explains: 'There is a band of self-appointed defenders of "our culture" who find it impossible to imagine authenticity as anything but hermetic, and contemporaneity as anything other than cultural betrayal.'

Meanwhile the young Rwandan audiences, who relish Kiyarwanda-language hip hop and rap and find its social commentary speaks *ukuri* [the truth], and the Cape Verdeans, who celebrate Sousa's multiform art in Portuguese and creole, have no problems in appropriating and making their own – as art has always done – new ideas which they find exciting and relevant and which they can mix fruitfully with the forms they have inherited from their elders. What delights me in this collection of articles is that we see a diverse range of artists and audiences who refuse those critical discourses that seek to restrict the acceptable palate of African performance in accordance with narrowly conceived ideas of how the dual concepts of 'African' and 'art' may 'legitimately' cohabit in twenty-first-century time and space.

ALEMSEGED TESFAI

# The Day Weki Burned

She loved binoculars. Every time she peered into their magic, she would snatch them away from her eyes and examine them carefully, muttering her utter fascination. Daytime guard duty was not a chore that the rest of the unit had to worry about. She would volunteer to take over everyone's turn, just to toy with our most precious possession.

On the morning that Weki burned, 13 March 1975, she and I had been left behind at the village of Dekemhare, some forty kilometers north of Asmara and about ten northwest of Weki itself. Ethiopian soldiers, 3,000 strong in 60 trucks, had entered the village very early that morning on their way to Fishey, down the forested eastern escarpment leading to the plains adjacent to the Red Sea coastline. Our unit leader had told us to follow developments from Dekemhare until the soldiers' return to Asmara. The unit was then responsible for the EPLF's administrative tasks of the area.

It was a lazy morning. I had nothing to do, nothing to read, and there was no one around for a meaningful discussion. I could not even break the monotony by taking the binoculars away from my comrade. She would not let go of them; neither would she ever tire of scanning the morning dryness of the hills, valleys, and plains sprawling between Dekemhare and Weki.

'*Wenbedie*,' she called out to me, as I drowsed on top of a *hidmo*, the traditional highland house, a few metres away from her. *Wenbedie* is Amharic for bandit or highway robber, her pet name for me. It was a derogatory word used by the Ethiopians to refer to Eritrean freedom fighters. She could not have been out of her teens yet. I was past thirty, the old man of the unit. But, there, she had a nickname for me. '*Wenbedie*, how can this thing bring that tree so far away right to my nose? How does it work?'

'You have asked me that before,' I replied with a yawn. 'It has to do with the shape of the glasses and the way they are placed in front of each other.'

'I know that. I want to know how the shape of the glasses and the way they are placed in front of each other bring far away objects to my nose.'

'I don't know how that is done.' I really did not know. I do not remember even now if I had ever come across binoculars in my few and long forgotten physics lessons, or wherever those gadgets were taught about.

'With all the plusses that you carry around, you don't know how this one works?' Plusses meant the number of years that one studied after high school. She loved to tease me about that. 'You reached the 20th Grade?' she would often say with exaggerated wonder. 'Why don't you give me five of them? You can still be happy with the remaining fifteen!'

'The plusses were about something else, not binoculars.'

'They are right what they say about you.' Her tone had changed to one of reproach.

'Who says what about me?' She did not respond. She continued to scan the countryside. I repeated the question, trying to maintain my cool.

'Never mind, it is not just about you, it is about all of you, the petty bourgeois.'

'All right, what do they say about me or the petty bourgeois?'

She gave me a quick sidelong glance. 'That you do not want to share your knowledge with us, that you don't want the masses to know what you know.'

I turned to look at her. She had gone back to the glasses. 'Do you really believe that I know about binoculars and that I don't want you to know what I know?'

'Maybe, you are a petty bourgeois, aren't you?'

'I suppose you can call me that.'

'So?'

'So?'

'So, if you are a petty bourgeois and if it is petty bourgeois nature to hide your knowledge, why should I not suspect that you don't want me to know how these binoculars work?'

Satisfied with her logic, she flashed a triumphant smile at me. Her face had not yet grown to fit her adult teeth; they sparkled big and snow white in the morning sun. Her tight shorts revealed strong peasant legs and sunburned thighs scarred and bruised by long marches and cuts from falls and thorny shrub. Her curly, uncombed hair covered half of her face, almost hiding enchanting dimples on both cheeks – a sturdy country girl with all the charm and lustre of youth, ravaged by the wilderness.

I got curious. I wanted to know more about what the unit thought of me and my fellow 'petty bourgeois'. I prodded on. 'That's not fair. You should not judge your comrades based on what you learn in political education lessons. Political education teaches broad ideas. You should judge your comrades from what they do and what you know about them.'

'All right, all right, stop. Forget about the binoculars. Maybe you really don't know. But there is something that I have observed about you that I don't like.'

'What?'

'You want to be different from us. When we play and joke, you just sit and watch us from a distance. You don't participate in the life of the masses. And then ... and then ... at night, when we sleep, we huddle up together, men and women, for warmth. You sleep away from us, alone even in the terrible cold of Zagir. I think that only petty bourgeois people do that.'

She was getting on my nerves. But I spoke with as much composure as I could muster. I had to. Getting angry did not pay with younger fighters, especially women. They were impressionable, quick to react, and most likely to raise the issue on the Wednesday afternoon criticism and self-criticism session of our unit. That was where every fault, chance remark, and every actual or perceived aberration and deviation was openly discussed and corrected. I was not keen on becoming the topic at the coming Wednesday as a result of this animated discussion with my sharp critic.

'Listen,' I said, abandoning my reclining position to sit up straight and face her. 'To begin with, I am much older than all of you, even the unit leader. I can't be jumping, kicking, and pulling someone's hair all the time. I am past that stage. Remember, I am almost old enough to be your father.'

'You are not that old. And what if you were? In our revolution, everyone is an equal. There is no age, sex, or class discrimination. That was the first thing we learned in the training camp. Maybe you missed it then.'

'Does the revolution teach us not to respect older people?'

'No.'

'Good. My age does not allow me to behave the way all of you youngsters do. You have to respect that.'

She frowned and after a pause said, 'I will think about it.'

'Let's talk about your second criticism. I cannot sleep within a crowd. I am not used to it. I cannot sleep with people on both sides of me, tossing and turning and breathing on my face. This has nothing to do with being petty bourgeois.'

'It does. That's not your real reason.'

'What is my real reason?'

'We believe in *tewdih*. *Tewdih* is a corruption of an Arabic word meaning 'telling it like it is'. 'I think you are afraid to sleep next to us because we are women. You would if you considered us your comrades. Real comrades are equals. The love between them is revolutionary. When I look at you, I see a comrade. But I don't think you have the same feelings about me or the other women in the unit. I suspect you see us the same way that you saw your women friends in Asmara. Sorry, but *tewdih* is *tewdih*.'

She upset me this time. 'You are passing limits, Comrade,' I said, wagging my forefinger at her. 'You are not going to give me a lesson on the relationship between men and women. You know very little about that because you are still too young. I encourage your comradely relationship with all of us. But stop giving political meaning to everything that I do. It is my business.'

She fell silent and went back to her binoculars. There was an element of truth in what she had said. I truly could not see myself rubbing bodies with pretty girls all night, albeit comrades in the revolution, and resisting for long an eventual inevitable submission to the demands of nature. But I marvelled, even envied, her total and unmitigated embrace of everything that the revolution taught. Here was a young woman, six months inside the Eritrean revolution, who believed that she had transcended the natural divide between men and women, just as she believed that she had risen above the other 'divides' – religion, class, regionalism. She probably was convinced that she had shut off all the glands, cut out the tissues, and closed down the entries and exits that nature has provided men and women for pleasure and procreation.

'How long will this conviction last?' I mused to myself. But I refrained from carrying the conversation further for fear of violating her innocence. I knew also that the revolution thrived on the unquestioning faith of the young in its ideals and principles. Tampering with that faith was therefore not in my book. So I went back to my reclining position and was about to resume my 'petty bourgeois' reveries, when she sprang to her feet with a shout.

'*Wenbedie!*' she cried out, quite agitated. 'I see smoke in the direction of Weki. Come and look.'

I took the binoculars and, indeed, a column of smoke was visible rising upwards at the tip of the escarpment to our southeast. 'Maybe it is a haystack, but I am not sure if it is Weki.'

'It is Weki. I know where it is, it is my village. I think we should go.'

She was already slinging her Senobal on to her shoulders and placing the binoculars in their box. The Senobal, a sensitive Israeli Uzi-type submachine gun, was the weapon of her choice. I never messed with that gun. It tended to release its contents if dropped or even banged against a hard surface. I was content with my hand grenade, a product of China.

I held her by the arm and told her that we could not leave yet. She would not listen. 'Look, *Wenbedie*,' she said, 'we cannot let those bastards burn down a whole village. Maybe our comrades there need our help.' She did not mention her family. In her mind, comrades came first. I too refrained from asking after them as she would probably have admonished me for harbouring bourgeois family sentiment.

'What can you and your Senobal and I and my hand grenade do to avert the situation? Besides,' I continued snatching the binoculars away from her and focusing on Weki, 'we don't know what exactly is happening out there or what there is between here and Weki.'

The column of smoke had now grown much thicker and blacker. Obviously, something bigger and much wider than a haystack was aflame. I was gripped by a mixture of anger, worry, and fear. But I felt that going there on impulse would be futile, possibly suicidal. So I insisted that we sent someone from the village for reliable information and just wait with patience.

Since the enemy did not leave the area that day, we were forced to spend the afternoon and the night in Dekemhare. All the time, she chided me for what she called my 'petty bourgeois caution and hesitancy'. 'We should not run away from danger, we should go to it,' she kept repeating over and over again. 'Otherwise, how will we win the war?' I took her anger and frustration with good humour. Although she was not saying it, I suspected that, deep inside, she was probably also concerned about her family and loved ones. I took care not to upset her.

★ ★ ★

News did not come until early afternoon the next day. As the huge enemy column approached Weki the previous morning, church bells had rung out in warning and EPLF units in the village had advised the inhabitants to evacuate to safety. Younger men, women, and children had heeded the call and cleared out to the forest down the escarpment nearby. But, suspecting reprisals for Weki's role in hosting freedom fighters coming up or going down the escarpment, the elderly had decided to appease the approaching soldiers by appearing to welcome them. And so they did – the priests in their colourful robes, carrying umbrellas and crosses; and the elders in their snow-white, hand-woven-cotton, toga-like shawls, the *netselas* and *gabis*, ready with an assortment of gifts.

What followed ranks with the most atrocious and senseless acts of cruelty perpetrated by Ethiopian soldiers on unprotected civilians. With no provocation whatsoever, our informants said, they shot into the mass of bodies welcoming them. About forty people died that morning. The soldiers then made the rounds in the village, purposely torching Weki's magnificent *hidmos*, some of the most spacious and artistic that I had ever seen anywhere in Eritrea. Many spent the night there to burn more houses and haystacks and to ransack households. By the time of their return to Asmara the next morning, Weki was no longer the place it had been.

I watched my companion as we were being told all this. She sat there impassive. If there were emotions rocking her inside, she did not show them.

On our way out of Dekemhare, we met a group of fighters coming from the opposite direction. They filled us in on some of the horrible details. Apparently, she knew one of them. She drew him aside and had an animated discussion with him before she rejoined me and we continued on our way. She looked flustered.

As the afternoon sun worked on both of us, I tried to keep in step with her quick and ever quickening pace. Throughout our work together, there was never a time when I could outpace her. But this time I walked level with her. We proceeded side by side for several minutes, not a word being uttered between us. I knew that something had gone wrong.

'Can we stop for a while?' I asked her.

'Why?'

'There is something you are not telling me. You are walking strangely and you are hurting the earth.' That was a joke between us, my way of telling her to tread more softly on the ground. That remark had always drawn a smile from her, not this time. 'All right, then,' I said, stopping her and forcing her to sit on a flat stone nearby. 'You tell me what is bothering you or we will not move from here. I mean it.'

She did as she was told. 'My father and his brother were among the forty or so who are dead.' Except for a slight frown, there was no expression on her face, no emotion in her voice. She could have been making an ordinary statement.

'*Mbwa'e!*' I exclaimed. 'Both of them?'

'Both of them. They were dumb and stupid, all of them. How could they trust those donkeys? They begged to be killed with their crosses and they got it. Maybe they will all go to heaven now.'

I could not believe or accept her attitude. 'How can you talk like that about your family?' I asked her, quite angry this time.

'My family is the revolution.'

'It is mine too. But the revolution does not tell me not to feel at least sorry for my father's death.'

'*Wenbedie*, what do you want me to do? Wail and scream as they do in the village? Pull my hair out? Do we cry when we bury our comrades? We don't. We say, "they have accomplished their mission". We say that about young people my age, our comrades who will die for us. Why do you want me to feel differently about a bunch of old people who found themselves where they should not have been, even if my father was one of them?'

Obviously, six months in the revolution had turned her into a fiery debater. She had also identified all the sentiments deemed counter-revolutionary and cleaned them out of her system, or so she believed. But I did not want to indulge her this time. I thought that she needed some redirection. At the same time, I had to be careful how I said it.

'Listen carefully and don't misunderstand me,' I told her earnestly. 'I am not asking you to put family sentiment over our revolutionary duties and dedication. All right?'

'All right, continue.' She was impatient.

'We are dedicated to the revolution because we love our country. Do you agree?'

'Yes.'

'Where did that love come from? From our parents.' I felt awkward in my own rhetoric. 'It is not possible to love your country without first loving your parents and neighbours and those who saw you grow up in the village.'

'So?' She did not look impressed at all.

'So we have to reserve some feelings for them. The way you just talked about your father is not something I can accept. He is not a stranger; he is not your enemy. He is your father.'

She gazed at me as if from a distance, her mouth twisted in an amused smile or a smirk, I was not sure which. She did not respond to my emotional speech. Instead, she collected her things, rose up, and resumed our trip without even glancing at me. I followed her, very angry, more with myself than with her. I debated alone on the wisdom of such dialogue with young fighters who were most likely to misunderstand, not only the kind of words that I had uttered, but also the whole message, my whole motive. I felt that I had just intruded upon a system of ideas and attitudes that I did not quite fit into. It was a strange feeling – to be a part and to belong, but not quite – a feeling that left a bad taste in my mouth.

After well over an hour's journey, we were only a few minutes away from Weki. Weki and Zagir are twin villages situated right at the tip of the beautiful eastern escarpment, the Semenawi Bahri. They had provided the arena for one of the bloodiest confrontations between the forces of the ELF and the EPLF only a few months earlier, in late 1974. But they will also be remembered for having hosted thousands of the supporters of both liberation fronts who placed themselves between the warring parties, demanding a peaceful solution to their differences. That bold move was to bear some fruit early in 1975.

I could see that my comrade was heading straight for Weki and not going, as I had thought, to Zagir, the EPLF headquarters of the area. I hastened to overtake her.

'Where are you going?' I asked blocking her way.

'I want to take a look at what those donkeys have done to the village.'

'I don't think it is a good idea.'

'Why not?'

'Because we don't know what to expect there. Our instruction is to go to Zagir and that is what we should do. Besides, it is better that the unit leader knows about this so he can decide if you can go to Weki at this time.'

'It is only a short distance from here to there.' She pointed to the adjacent villages that seem to meet at the edges. 'If you are afraid I might die of shock, I will not. Or, if you can't stand the sight of burnt houses and dead bodies, wait for me here. I will run in and rejoin you in a few minutes.'

She was only one month my senior in the revolution, but she was teasing me again. I stopped insisting and gave in to her wish. Maybe it was best that she went in. I followed her.

★ ★ ★

The Weki cemetery is situated to the west of the village. It borders the road that branches off the Keren-Asmara highway and that leads to the escarpment. I could see several new graves out of the corner of my eye, probably those of the victims of the previous morning. I cringed at the thought that my companion's father and uncle occupied two of those hastily covered mounds of earth. But she did not even glance that way. She was intent on going to a specific place, possibly her father's *hidmo*. We entered Weki.

My heart sank when I saw the rubble that the best of the village had been reduced to. Only a few weeks before, I had stood in front of three *hidmos* in particular, admiring their architectural finesse. They each had twelve wooden pillars supporting a cylindrical roof of perfect symmetry. I had an afternoon all to myself that day and I had spent it in the cool shade of one of the verandahs. All three were now gone along with dozens of others. What was left of most of those houses were the charred stone walls and the smoldering fire under ashes mixed with debris from the capsized roofs. One fallen pillar was still emitting smoke.

She led me up narrow and steep paths to the higher parts of Weki, closer to the tip of the escarpment. Several huts and *hidmos* were still standing and I could hear lone voices wailing from inside some of them. The smell of burning flesh, human or animal I could not tell, churned my stomach. I passed an old man and a woman who were staring at a destroyed *hidmo* in total helplessness and resignation. They appeared too numbed by the catastrophe even to cry. Their still life pose stays with me even now, over three decades later. Weki, its houses charred, its honour violated, and its inhabitants scattered for the moment, was all numbness.

I was fighting the nausea inside me when she led me to an open space towards the northern edge of the village. She stopped abruptly, staring at a fair-sized *hidmo* burned down to the ground. It had a large well-maintained compound. The haystack to the right was now fine ashes rising and blowing away in the gentle afternoon breeze.

'That's our house,' she whispered in a hoarse voice. She started for the compound, but I restrained her, calling out to the neighbouring unharmed houses for someone to appear. We struggled a little, but I held her tightly. 'The bastards!' she kept cursing, 'Beasts! Donkeys!' She was clutching her hair, pressing her temples, and beating her chest as she rained insults on the perpetrators of the atrocity. I called out repeatedly.

An old woman appeared from somewhere behind the compound. She was so covered in dust and soot from head to feet that she seemed to have just risen from the ashes. As she cupped her hand over her eyes for closer inspection, my comrade recognized her aunt and let out a frighteningly deafening shriek. Momentarily stunned by the old woman's ghostly image, I was not ready for the shove that sent me staggering. Before I could stop her, my comrade had hurled her Senobal to one side, sent the binoculars flying to the other, and dropped to a kneeling position. She spread her hands as if in prayer and stayed there for several minutes, motionless. She was probably fighting against the contradictory emotions inside her. I let her be.

It took a few minutes for the full impact of what had just happened to sink into her. The old aunt was already circling the compound, calling on the deceased to come back and welcome their daughter. The Tigrinya dirge is a tear-jerker even under the circumstances of everyday funerals. The aunt was wailing in a sing-song voice with a quiver on the high note. I was moved to tears, but the effect on her niece was more immediate and violent.

Involuntary tears had already been washing down her plump cheeks. She crouched in a kneeling position and started sobbing, her voice breaking in intermittent hiccups. I drew near to touch her hair and attempt to console her, but she shook my hand off, letting out a scream of sorrow and rage. Her sobs and hiccups grew in strength and intensity, and she started convulsing as if gripped in an epileptic seizure. She dropped to the ground, beat the earth, scattered dust into the air and called on both her parents to appear for just one moment. Apparently, her mother had died years earlier. She was not calming down. On the contrary, she got hysterical.

In a panic, I ran to her and shook her by the shoulders, but she kept on shaking and screaming. I told the aunt to stop crying and fetch some water. Alarmed, she ran towards her hut. In the meantime, the convulsions were not letting up. I shook her repeatedly, calling on her to come back to her senses. She did not respond. So I landed two slaps, forehand and backhand, on her dimpled cheeks. She sat up, startled. By then, the aunt had given me a large tin of water. I splashed some on her face and poured the rest on top of her head. She came to.

She sprang back to her feet as abruptly as she had fallen on her knees. She paused for a moment and said, 'Where is my Senobal?' I fetched it from where it had been lying and handed it to her. 'And the binoculars?' I gave her those too. The old aunt was attempting to hug and console her. She was not paying much attention. Without looking at either one of us, she used her shawl to remove dust from the gun and the binoculars holder.

'Let's go,' she ordered as soon as she was ready. She started to move, turning away from her father's compound and her weeping aunt. She did not look back.

The sun had set, but it was not dark yet. As we approached Zagir, she stopped to face me. 'Why did you slap me like that?' she asked. There was no anger in her voice.

'You were hysterical. You were passing out. I had to.'

She turned to resume walking, but turned back again. '*Wenbedie*, if you talk to anyone about what you saw in Weki today, if you tell on me, I will empty the bullets in my Senobal into your body. I mean it.'

Her dimple deepened as she looked at me with a smile of slight embarrassment that could not conceal the relief of a good cry. I too smiled at her, grateful that her perceptions and interpretations of revolutionary culture had not dulled her sense of sympathy and humanity.

I did not tell on her.

★ ★ ★

Although I did not see her for a long time after that, I had no problem following her progress. She had become, not surprisingly, a famous warrior and a leader of both women and men.

I met her again only once in the early eighties at a field hospital. She was weaning her newly-born baby. When she saw me, we broke into simultaneous laughter. The dimples were still there, but her face had finally matured to fit her teeth.

'Do you remember what I said to you the day that Weki burned?' she asked as she handed me the baby to rock for a while. 'I really never thought then that this one would ever come.' She was shaking her head, laughing and marvelling at her new status of motherhood.

'Times do change, don't they? And with them, perceptions.'

'I did not know that at the time.'

I switched the topic. 'I never told anyone about that scene you made at your house in Weki.'

'I know. I would have killed you if you had, *Wenbedie*.' She laughed again and then grew serious. 'When I saw the stone where my father used to sit to wash his feet after a hard day's work, I could not control myself.'

'Have you cried since that day?'

'Only twice, all by myself, when special comrades died. Have you cried here, *Wenbedie*?'

'No, it has been six years and not a drop. I want to sometimes, but I can't.' I switched the topic again. 'Do you think motherhood will change you?'

'She is the daughter of the revolution,' she answered taking the baby back to her bosom. 'I will rejoin my company as soon as she stops breast-feeding. I will fight the same way I did before she came.' She smiled tenderly at the sleeping baby, enjoying motherhood while it lasted.

We said our farewells and expressed our hopes to meet upon final victory.

We never did. She died in the line of duty, in one of the battles of the mid-eighties.

## OKINBA LAUNKO

# Two Trees Came Into My Garden

IN MEMORIAM KOFI AWOONOR

Some five years ago, respected elder Kofi Awoonor, you kindly cut down
at my request two stems of a tree in your garden, for me to take home and
plant in my own house here in Ibadan …

And I have watched them grow since,
Rapidly, as you promised – two mermaids
Of green luxuriant hair rising up from prayer gaily,
And stretching their arms out in immemorial pose
To catch the jewels of dawn, and the stars of night,
And the grains of sun-fall in-between –

Ah, in my turn I too gave my word
To bring you here one of these days to sit
In the shade of these trees and listen
To the echo of your wisdom-mellowed words,
The nuggets that enrich my solitude …

And now you are gone! So suddenly
And in a quarrel you knew little about!
The termites of hate, in human guise,
Have left us bereft with their callous guns
Giving us no chance to say our goodbyes,
But knowing nothing of these trees

Which continue to wave their hands
And laugh at their vanity, these new seekers
Of peace who would willingly waste children's lives
In their virtuous quest for justice!
See, my trees flaunt their hair as proof

That no bomb or bullet can kill a poem:
Each leaf unfolds the syllables of your voice,
Each stem an assurance that your metaphors
Will never cease to grow and to flourish
In the gardens of our grateful hearts.

Two trees came into my garden
With your blessing, Elder One:
Two poems now to cherish forever.

Ibadan. 26 September 2013

# Alone Onstage

## MÁRIO LÚCIO SOUSA

TRANSLATED FROM THE PORTUGUESE BY CHRISTINA S. McMAHON AND
EUNICE S. FERREIRA IN CONSULTATION WITH CARLOS ALMEIDA AND JEFF HESSNEY

Solo piece for an actress.

**Characters:**
The Mrs
The Maid
The Nanny
The Priest
The Uncle
The Niece

**Setting:**
The various household environments of the characters. In general, there should be the sense of an affluent house with two interior doors adjacent to each other, which can easily open and close.

*The play opens with the silhouette of a woman writing.*

OFFSTAGE VOICE: I am writing this, even though I am illiterate; or rather, I pretend that I write, because I don't have anything to tell; or maybe I do. Because everybody has something to tell. And also to count: fingers and toes, highs and lows, scratchings on a wall, pies in the sky, tall tales, long-tailed magpies, facts, contracts, dreams, financial schemes, footsteps, insects … but my own story isn't very interesting. Could it be that I actually have a story? If my uncle were alive, this is what he might write: 'Hey Mário,[1] how's it going? I've read and re-read the play and I don't understand its line of action, what story you want to tell. I don't understand the theme. I find the characters unclear and I don't understand their function. What do they add to the narrative? What would make people want to hear this story? What would captivate them about it? Also, the dialogues depart from dramatic writing and drift into a more narrative style. I wish you had more time to work on the text. What makes the woman so special that her story deserves to be told, and, more importantly, to be heard? What's her conflict? What will she leave behind in the people who listen to her?'

*Blackout.*

*We hear chimes from a grandfather clock. It sounds expensive and rich — just like the people who live here. Lights up. An older woman enters alone but as if she is speaking to someone.*

THE MRS: (*Her manner is classy, somewhere between confident and suspicious. Still busy dressing herself for work, she is both questioning her new domestic servant and showing her the various rooms in the house, constantly entering and leaving the scene.*) What is your name? (*She feigns that she hears a reply, and responds with a slight bow.*) Maria. Maria. (*She enquires as she walks.*) Maria, as in Marie Antoinette? This is the dining room, and there's the TV room. Maria Rilfe?[2] Here is the master bedroom, and that is our bathroom. Maria, like Mary Magdalene? Here's my husband's office, the library, which is his bedroom when he has insomnia, and it will be our son's room, but that's the future, in the future; another bathroom. Maria Callas?[3] Here is the patio, another bathroom, yours; at your disposal, an ironing room (*clarifying*) for starching and straightening. Maria Bethânia?[4] Here is the porch, another bathroom. Maria, like Mary Pope?[5] (*Opens a door and disappears; from offstage.*) Here is the kitchen: everything for making lunch is in there. (*Enters.*) Maria, like Anne-Marie, Queen of Greece?[6] You'll clean from 8 to 10, and from 10 to noon you will prepare lunch. In the afternoon, you'll do the ironing. Maria, Maria, Maria de Walter?[7] From today on, the house is under your command. (*Turns to the maid.*) Take good care of it. Good care, because you know (*making air quotes with her fingers*) 'even a private house is a component of the Empire'. My husband dixit.[8] Ta-ta for now. (*She leaves. We hear the door close.*)

*The Maid enters timidly and curiously through the same door. At first glance, she doesn't appear to have any sense of humor. She has a sober air, serious and pure, yet she is tender and actually a natural comic. She cranes her neck in various directions as though she is looking for something, and to make sure that no one else is in the house.*

THE MAID: Maria. Maria, yes. Maria Aparecida da Silva. Aparecida from her mother's side and Silva from her father's. Born on the island of São Nicolau in 1947. Not married, not single, not widowed. Orphaned by her father and mother, raised by her dear Uncle Dessidério. After that, a servant – an indentured servant in São Tomé.[9] And now, thank God, also a servant – to Mr and Mrs Empire. But Maria. (*Beats her hand against her chest.*) Proudly Maria, like all servants, like the mother of Jesus, because she also was a servant to the Holy Spirit for nine months.

(*Begins to familiarize herself with all of the corners of the house.*) Empire, what a name! La-di-da. Only rich people could afford a name like Empire. In São Tomé I also knew families called Empire, and Vituperation, and my neighbor, Judgement, all of them related. The only one missing was Grave. Grave, yes … that is one last name that gathers all God's children into the same family. (*Remembers and imitates with seriousness the descriptions provided by the Mrs.*) 'Here is the master bedroom, and that is our bathroom.' So here is where Mr and Mrs Empire make (*rubs her index fingers together*) the future. And my job is to make the bed so that the Future is sweet, chubby, healthy, and bursting with joy. (*Looks at a picture frame.*) Oh, how handsome, Mr Empire with a hat and tie, ooh, with emblems, how elegant! Mr Empire was so stylish as a young man. (*Another photograph.*) Mrs Empire with a bikini, oh, how beautiful. It's a shame that the bikini is not what it used to be. People used to be so innocent. In my opinion, the bikini has no future, poor bikini. Back in the days, we were a lot more peaceful.

*She imitates a primary school teacher.*

Do you all know what a Bikini is? You know, people have a habit of using things they don't know the first thing about. Bikini is one of the Marshall Islands – from Micronesia, in the Pacific Ocean. It was there that the Americans tested the first atomic bombs. Today it is a still life. Do you understand?

*She goes back to being herself.*

I didn't understand anything. Here is Mr and Mrs Empire's bathroom. It's not dirty, but I still have to clean it. It's the kind of dirt you don't see, just like the Bikini. It appears to be totally spotless. But it's dirty. And of course it is, because if the Future is going to be born in a clean atmosphere, I have to do the work. (*She enters the bathroom and disappears.*) (*From offstage*) Ah, the ocean, it's like music. It's there, but if you touch it, it's not the ocean anymore, it's just water. It's not even blue; it has no color. It slips away from people. But the ocean is only there for us to listen to and dance to. And to be afraid of.

*The actress re-enters the scene as the Nanny.*

THE NANNY: (*turns and shouts back toward the bathroom*) Be careful, Future, don't slip. Everything my uncle Dessidério taught me I'm going to teach Future. After all, you need to be brave to birth a child, but you gotta be crazy to raise one … (*shouting*) hold on, child (*muttering*) I can't find your diaper, can't find your toys, can't find anything. So I guess I'll dress you like a sunflower. (*Picks up a child's outfit covered with sunflower patterns and handles it like a child, in a moment of deep tenderness.*) Your old Auntie Nanny[10] knows that the sun revolves around children, and that it comes in slyly to hide in the dimples of their eyes at nap-time, after their bath and their snack. You'll see how the bees will sing your praises, because I know that bees and butterflies live for tomorrow. This is what Uncle Dessidério taught your old Auntie Nanny: bees are not like spiders that live suspended in time and don't know when it's dawn or night-time. Since they're creatures that weave, they weave in the night. Spiders weave, but they don't dream. Uncle Dessidério used to say that they do dream, they just don't remember, because memories get them tangled up. But bumblebees do, bees dream, they spend their whole lives dreaming because they always live for tomorrow. They're like the blind, although blind people only dream in the dark, but they do dream everything: light, colors, things, beauty, clouds. We had a blind person in our village. He used to say that what confused him most was the skyline. Uncle Dessidério used to say, 'the blind are not like bats, who always dream in the dark and about the dark. The blind dream just like us.' Don't you think it's sad for someone to have webs but never a loom? I think it's sad. But bees … they only dream about flowers. You're going to dream about flowers too, Future, soon you'll be spinning tops, then you'll learn to sing, then to spell things as if you had a fountain of words in your head, you'll have a pen that oozes greetings, that gives people news, that tells secrets, that spouts knowledge, writes all the basic things, you're also going to have your own Future, and that Future will have his own. And you will teach him that we make the future *from* the future, isn't that right, child? You'll be cut loose by then. Mrs and Mr Empire won't be around, ordering you to take your finger out of your mouth, your nose, your ears, your peepee. Sure, older people think that we wring the future out from the present, but that's not it at all. The child that never stumbles never learns to fall, and then when he grows up, he sinks and spends his whole life shipwrecked. And then we die, child. Because you know there aren't any otters on earth, otters only live in the sea, the ocean, an ocean with freshwater right in the middle of it, because weasels only drink freshwater, and they like warm water … warm water (*the word brings to her mind something forgotten, but it takes a while for her to remember*) warm water (*screams, and runs for the bathroom*). Exits.

*She returns as the Maid, busy as ever with household tasks.*

THE MAID: (*shaking her head and looking thoughtful*) Hot water, wow, hot water like it was born right there in the tap. Did they leave some kind of heater on, or is that faucet broken? Could it be that instead of a water tank on the roof, Mr and Mrs Empire have a wood-burning stove pumping smoke into the sky? Making steam? I swear, these people, the more money they have, the crazier they are. I saw that in São Tomé. A bunch of butt-naked people laying out in the sun getting sunburned (*makes the sign of the cross on herself*). Goodness. If it was just warm water … But, dammit, water that comes out of the tap boiling hot with smoke and everything! So strange. Not even my Uncle Dessidério would know how to explain this! What do Mr and Mrs Empire *do* with water that comes out of the faucet so hot? Could it be that they're scalding themselves so they can stay young?[11] For the love of God, really? I'm gonna go turn that thing off. (*Still lost in thought, she drifts off toward another room. She ducks her head out of the scene, then re-enters imitating the Mrs with solemnity and respect.*) 'Here is my husband's office, the library, which is his bedroom when he has insomnia, and it will be our son's room; another bathroom.' Another bathroom? (*She seems amazed for a moment, but suddenly becomes convinced.*) Another bathroom? Ahh … Same thing you do with two washbasins. Wash dirty clothes in one and fill the other one with clean water. Okay, sure. I'll scrub. My job is to clean, so the Future will not … (*Suddenly she lifts up her head in fascination.*) My God, so many books … What does Mr Empire do with all of these? My God, it reminds me of my Uncle Dessidério. But too many words are probably bad for the stomach. He should take it easy and just give all those kooky and confusing words in his head a rest. It's like crazy old Rosa the Crooner said: time is one discount we're all entitled to get.[12] Ave Maria! Words shouldn't cost so much. Or else the cost should only be for those who write them, not those who buy them. Who in the world can afford to buy so many words?

My Uncle Dessidério had this huge book just full of words. He said it was about the life of Gago 'The Stutterer' Coutinho.[13] I laughed just looking at the cover. If the guy was a stutterer, how did he say so many words? But I never asked Uncle Dessidério what that guy said. I used to think it was Coutinho himself who put all those words down in a book so that he wouldn't stammer over them when he needed to say them. But now I know that stutterers will sputter around even when trying to s-say their own n-name.

*Stands still. She's going more and more into her reminiscences. She begins to act out a little girl about five years of age.*

THE NIECE: Uncle told me that when I turn six years old he's going to teach me to read. But he can read, and I can listen. I'll dust the books for Uncle, and Uncle will read them to me. Right?

*Goes to look for a book. Begins to act out a man of about 50 years of age. Walks with a book in his hand. He is fat, wears a cap, and sniffs snuff. He is restless and is always looking for something. He speaks with a smile. He plays mischievously with his niece, the little girl, gives milk to the cat, and does dozens of household errands without ever looking up from his book.*

THE UNCLE: (*busy with tasks*) Words give themselves away, my niece, they are not sold. I was born on the island of São Nicolau. (*Reading.*) 'One of the chief causes that can be assigned for the curiously commonplace character of most of the literature of our age is undoubtedly the decay of lying as an art, a science, and a social pleasure.' (*Still busy with tasks.*) I was a scholar[14] and a Notary Public. Now I am a widower and retired and diabetic and asthmatic. (*Reading.*) 'The ancient historians gave us delightful fiction in the form of fact; the modern novelist presents us with dull facts under the guise of fiction.'[15] (*Closes the book and gives himself over to his tasks.*) Who? Who do you think it could be? Oscar Wilde, the great Wilde, what a fucking poet! But now I'm going to urinate (*drags his feet in the direction of one of the rooms, enters and closes the door, thus disappearing from the scene*).

THE MAID/THE NIECE: (*from offstage*) No, no, please! I just cleaned the toilet.

THE UNCLE: (*opens the door and pokes out his head*) I swear I won't go poop.

THE MAID/THE NIECE: (*pokes out her head through the adjacent, half open door, like someone who needs light in order to make something out; holds up a book to the light; pinches her nose with her other hand and complains*) Hmm, hmm: smells like …

THE UNCLE: (*opens the adjacent door and appears there reading on the toilet*) Baudelaire: 'Je suis belle, ô mortels! Comme un rêve de pierre.'[16] (*Closes the door; from offstage.*) 'Et mon sein, où chacun s'est meurtri tour à tour.'[17]

*The Niece appears at the adjacent door, the one to the office.*

THE NIECE: If I only knew how to read, like my Uncle Dessidério.[18] (*Holds up the book with one hand, and caresses her breast with the other one. Imitates, with great concentration, the image she has of her uncle reciting poems.*)
> 'And my breast where each one in turn has bruised himself
> Is made to inspire in the poet a love
> As eternal and silent as matter.'

*Goes into the other door, the one to the bathroom, innocently picking up her skirt at the back and sitting on the toilet. Remembers her uncle.*

> 'On a throne in the sky, a mysterious sphinx,
> I join a heart of snow to the whiteness of swans;'

*Closes the door poetically.*

THE NIECE: (*reading from offstage*)
> 'I hate movement for it displaces lines,
> And never do I weep and never do I laugh.'

*We hear the sound of a man's loud outburst of laughter. Uncle Dessidério opens the bathroom door and is sitting on the toilet.*

THE UNCLE: 'Les poétes …' (*Becomes silent.*) That can be translated like this:

> Poets, before my grandiose poses,
> Which I seem to assume from the proudest statues,
> Will consume their lives in austere studies;

THE NIECE: (*shouting from offstage*) Uncle Dessidério, close the door.

THE UNCLE: (*opens the door; closes the book in an exaggerated fashion and dialogues with the cover*) The door to the soul. Whoever does not know how to read lives in the jungle. Whoever does not read is in a cage. (*Closes the door.*)

*The doorbell rings.*

THE NIECE: (*from offstage*) Uncle Dessidério, open the door!

THE UNCLE: (*opens the door brusquely; reopens the book and continues to read*) 'In that marvelous time in which Theology/Flourished with the greatest energy and vigor,/It is said that one day a most learned doctor/– After winning by force the indifferent hearts,/Having stirred them in the dark depths of their being;/After crossing on their way to celestial glory,/Singular and strange roads, even to him unknown,/Which only pure Spirits, perhaps, had reached, –/Panic-stricken, like one who has clamored too high/He cried, carried away by a satanic pride …'[19] (*Taps his face with the book.*)

THE NIECE: Uncle Dessidério, please! Close the door.

*Uncle Dessidério closes the door brusquely. We hear the doorbell ring again. He opens the restroom door, pours a bucket of water in the basin, and leaves adjusting his pants.*

THE UNCLE: I'm going. (*He takes his time going between one door and the next, muttering the whole time.*) Praying, defecating, reading, and copulating require concentration, dedication … I would even say a certain devotion, for the pleasure to be complete and the heights reached. One can't accept any disturbances. (*Leaves the stage by the door adjacent to the restroom; from offstage.*) Oh, it's you, sir. Make yourself at home. What news has brought you here, Father?

THE PRIEST: (*enters holding a book in his hand; walks on tiptoe, as if recoiling from someone right in front of his nose*) Your friend Baudelaire. (*Pronounces the French exaggeratedly.*) Forgive us, but bad faith has its limits. Why is this underlined? Is it because you underlined it, Dessidério, my friend? (*Reciting it like a homily.*) 'In that marvelous time in which Theology/

Flourished with the greatest energy and vigor,/ It is said that one day a most learned doctor'/, et cetera, et cetera, 'Panic-stricken, like one who has clamored too high/ He cried, carried away by a satanic pride,/ 'Jesus, little Jesus! I raised you very high!/ But had I wished to attack you through the defect in your armor,/your shame would equal your glory/ And you would be no more than a despised fetus.'[20] (*Raises his hands to his lips in a frenzy.*) Pssst. Don't apologize, Dessidério, my friend. A priest is a priest like a cat is a beast. My function here ... Pssst, not a peep. Yes, it is true that Baudelaire also talks about cats, which is underlined here by you as well, sir. (*Reciting.*) 'At a time when Nature with a lusty spirit,/ Was conceiving monstrous children each day,/ I should have liked to live near a young giantess,/ Like a voluptuous cat at the feet of a queen.'[21] Voluptuous cat, Dessidério, sir. I know that you're a communist, but don't create problems for me, my dear friend. Remember that when you die I am the one who will send your soul somewhere. Do you know where I typically send the communists?[22] Do me the favor of trading in this book. I do not want any French types around here because they were always very perverse, the Marquis de Sade, Napoleon, Lautrec ...[23] (*Begins to exit.*) Pssst! And that Joan of Arc is another one ... (*The priest reverses his route through the house, walking backwards as if he were rewinding, wagging his finger the whole time.*) That's right, I have stated my case, but first send the little girl to the nuns at the church. They can give her a decent education.

*He exits by the same door he entered. We hear the door close.*

THE UNCLE: (*poking his head out through the doorway*) I am not going to ruin Maria. And when I die, I do not want priests at my burial. You hear that? (*He hides himself once again.*)

THE MAID: (*screams from offstage*) Holy shit, what is this? Holy Mary Mother of God, what *is* this?

*The Maid emerges with a huge book in her hand, holding it up to the light to certify its content. Looks for a chair to sit down and reads the book, all the while letting out a creative string of profanities.[24] She sits there as if coming undone, scandalized but curious. She puts the book on the floor and begins to flip through its pages.*

THE MAID: Ai-yai-YAI! Ai-yai-YAI!!![25]

*The Maid tries to imitate positions from the Kama Sutra. However, she ends up looking like a cross between a Punjab dancer and a pornographic model, leading the audience to various interpretations of what she might be doing. She begins an earnest dance inspired by the Kama Sutra. From time to time she stops, catches her balance, and acts normally. Little by little, as she moves through various positions, she removes her head scarf, fans herself with an open hand, lets her hair loose, unbuttons her blouse, struts around the house, removes her apron and finally, falls exhausted into a chair.*

THE MAID: I am hot! Oh my God, I am hot! (*Takes off her long underwear.*) Now (*referring to the book*) this here looks like how the World began. Whew, I'm still hot. Okay, if this is how it all began, that's fine by me. (*Pausing to really take a good look at the book.*) No, it's the end of the World – but if this is how it's meant to be, I don't mind. Holy Mary Mother of God, what kind of book is this? Must be older than the Bible. I don't know if it's good or if it's bad – but what torture. Torture! Is this how Adam and Eve learned how to read? Sweet Jesus, it's sad not knowing how to read. What *is* this? How do you read this? (*She tries to sound out the title Ka-ma Su-tra in a comprehensible manner. She plays with the word 'Sutra' in a variety of ways.*) My uncle died and didn't keep his promise about teaching me how to read. Poor thing. (*Lost in thought, she recalls the past.*) I remember how the other women working on the plantation thought I was very bright.[26] 'Why is it that Maria does not know how to read?' they'd always ask. Maria doesn't know how to read because she took too long to turn six years old and her Uncle Dessidério didn't wait. (*Back to her senses.*) Well, it's a good thing anyhow. But seriously, what kind of book is this? It's a temptation! I will never touch it again. I'll be much better off for never again giving into this temptation. If this is how Mr and Mrs Empire are learning how to create the Future, I'll have a job for a long time.

*She shuts the book and rises. She holds up her long underwear to make it look like the legs of a child: running, jumping, tripping.*

A carefree, happy future that flows like water down a river. A future with no fear of getting hurt, a future that dances, that looks up at the world from the bottom up to the top, and not from the top to the bottom, because only God in heaven has that right. I don't really have to think about it because my voice doesn't matter anyhow. But I think that everyone should build a future just like they do in this book – really connected with each other. I'm just going to take one more little peak. *She opens the book, places it on the floor, and starts to dance again, but this time using her long underwear as a dance partner. She turns the pages of the book with her feet while recreating suggestive poses – never before seen poses representing the physical possibilities of copulating with her own undergarment: entwining the legs, placing her arms, head, a leg, inside the long underwear. Placing the garment over her shoulders, she rides it around. She continues to make more absurd and striking images.*

(*Exhausted and excited*) No, no. I don't want to see any more!

*She is disoriented. She returns the book to the Empire's library. She looks around the whole house for something to do. Suddenly, she stops. She takes a seat in front of the television and begins clicking through channels with the remote control.*

Yes, this will help me forget. Television. (*Frenetically clicks the remote control.*) This thing just goes on and on and on! (*Suddenly, she responds with a gesture of surprise. She watches for a while in silence, transfixed by what she sees.*) What is this? I don't understand. This man here says that he is going to disarm that one there and do it with all those weapons? This is confusing. If the person with the biggest dog is considered the strongest on the block, then all the neighbors will want a dog. And a pure bred, too, because not just any old mutt will last a good fight. What I would like to know is who was the first one to let the dog out? Who? Probably that guy who looks really afraid. I just don't get any of this. God, what will happen? (*Astonishment, fear, and sympathy.*) My God, what is this? Are people really able to do this? (*Starts counting on her fingers.*) I was born two years after. It was the year of the famine. Did that happen in Japan? Japan? Just like those little Japanese people from the Mindelo port?[27] Poor things. But who did this to them? Dear God, what did they do to deserve such a punishment? This is not God's punishment, this is Man's. Christ, what is this? Who was capable of doing something like this? Not even locusts do this! No, I can't bear to see so many cadavers. (*Changing the channel.*) Soccer, no. Horses? Again, no. Another war? No. And I do not like missiles. Oooh, but I do like 'Misses'.[28] Those pageant girls are so pretty. (*Seems to get bored while watching.*) But I have to get back to work. (*Imitating Mrs Empire.*) 'From 10 to noon you will prepare lunch.'

*She heads over to another section of the house but leaves the television on, taking occasional peeks while she works.*

(*From the kitchen.*) Onions, baby onions, beans, lard, cabbage, and hot sauce … (*Something on television piques her interest and she stands right in front of it while starting to repeat what she sees and hears.*) I … am … Carmen, I am … Venezuelan. I would like to end with (*not understanding*) with what? My hearing is good but I didn't understand that part. If only I had been able to go to school … (*imitating*) … La vida es … muy dura para las mujeres …, para las … mujeres, aqui (*she accentuates and points to her pelvis*) aqui en Venezuela, Vene … (*starts thinking very hard about something*) Vene … zuela, Vene … zuela, Vene … (*runs to the kitchen*).

(*From the kitchen. She hesitates as if trying to remember something.*) Vene, vene … vanilla! Rice, rice, rice, spice. Ham, ham, ham, yam. Eggs, eggs, chicken legs. (*Sticks her head out.*) I am going to make a *cachupa* like Mr and Mrs Empire have never eaten before.[29] A cachupa to put a baby in anyone's belly. Because we can't let baby Future go hungry! A weak Future is a sick Future. If he can't walk on his own two legs, he can't walk to school. I'm going to tell this to Mrs Empire: Deny yourself a good cachupa today, and you deny yourself a Future. (*Takes a peak at the television and then returns to watch some more.*) Ah? Je … suis … la … misse Frronce. Oh my God, why are there so many r's? Huh?

(*She exaggerates a French accent while heading back to the kitchen.*) Rrrrrrice, sugarrr, flourrr, baking powderrr (*in the kitchen*) Liberrrté, parrrrsley, waterrrcrrress, Frrraternité, safrrrron, grrrrain. (*Re-enters cutting an onion and wiping her eyes.*) But what I really love are onions. Onions are the eyes of the Earth. Eyes that God gave the Earth so she could cry for the poor. If onions did not exist, it would rain from the bottom up, from earth up to heaven. Thanks to the onion, we don't have rivers running in place of where there are clouds. And we don't have rivers flowing up the sides of mountains to the summits. I learned this in São Tomé: 'When there are no more onions, the world will end.'

(*She peeks at the television. Surprised and happy she listens to an announcement about training for actresses.*) Oh, look! Ah, this is what I want to be: an actress. If only I knew how to read. An actress. An actress of the theatre. Theatre is better than life because you can rehearse, erase, mess up, go back, and fix a mistake. I wanted to do theatre before Uncle Dessidério passed away. But it was a church play and he wouldn't let me. He said that kind of theatre was too over the top and a waste of my time. But, I liked it.

(*She imitates a bad actress reciting.*) 'Because the theatre records the memories of the future.' That's how I feel. (*Pause.*) 'As actors, we recall the child that we once were and can once again be.' (*Pause.*) 'An actor is someone inside of someone else who pretends to be another person in order to deceive the actor and the other person.' That's what I think, anyway. (*Pause.*) If only I could live as Maria and die an actress, ah, if only I could. (*Pause.*) At the end of someone's life, people cry. At the end of a play, people applaud. I like that. (*Pause.*) Applaud, even when the play is a piece of shit. Because it's a beautiful thing to do. Like at the races: I love to applaud everyone who crosses the finish line, not just the ones who get there first. (*Pause.*) Applaud, applaud …

*She begins to spin in circles, trance-like, dreaming while seeking or inciting applause. After a while of turning with arms wide open – as if she is lit by the moon – she stops but continues in a dream-like state. This time she fully gives herself over to fantasy as she imagines herself as an actress auditioning for a training program. She is in a theatre to audition. She is surrounded by technicians hanging lights, stage props, in short, all the theatrical paraphernalia needed to prepare the scenery for a play that will premiere later that day. The actress-candidate is happy to take orders, accommodate herself to others in the space, stay out of the way, etc …*

(*Stepping off the stage and feeling very shy, she speaks to the audience.*) Oh? Is this for me? All this applause is for me. Yes, Maria. I am Maria. Maria what? Maria. Marie Antoinette. MariaRilfe. Maria. Mary Magdalene. Maria Callas. Maria Bethânia. Maria Pope. Anne-Marie, Queen of Greece. Maria, Maria, Maria de Walter. Is it my turn now? (*As if talking to members of an audition jury.*) Excuse me, but I was watching television at the house where I work when I saw that you needed actresses – so I came. I don't know how to read or write but I have a very good memory. (*Fidgety, nervous and laughing.*) Okay, okay. Stay here? Where? You want me to go up there? (*She returns to the stage, fidgeting and muttering.*) And what do I do? Oh, no. Act? By myself? Me, all alone on a stage? No. Just me alone onstage? No. (*Looks from one side to the other…*) No. I'm too embarrassed. I don't want to. No. No, thank you.

*The silhouette of a woman writing.*

If I knew how to write, this is what I would have written about: My first day as a maid. Not for what I did that day, but for what I did not do. All because I didn't want to see myself alone onstage. And now here I am, alone in life. Alone, with my memories.

## Note from the Translators

Our approach to the translation of *Sozinha no palco* has been rooted in the hope that an English translation of the play will lead to production by theatre artists whose audiences do not understand Portuguese. While academic study of plays has its merit, our primary guiding principle has been to create a theatrical space for Cape Verdean performance to come to life on Anglophone stages. In addition to our scholarly research on Cape Verdean theatre, we also draw upon our varied experiences as performers, directors, and dramaturgs to imagine the play in production. The reader may note that the play is written in the style of American English as we have attempted to translate the essence of the multiple characters via general linguistic and expressive practices more familiar to our own target audiences. There are some instances when we have taken some liberties in order to best capture Sousa's clever wordplay. We hope that our language choices will allow Sousa's quirky writing style to shine through our translation, allowing it to be easily performed by other speakers of English around the globe.

The overall tone of the play invites directors and performers to draw upon a mixture of styles in production, including farce, absurdist drama, serious drama, and the enthralling, transformative nature of one-person performances. The Maid (or Maria) is the central character of the play and it is she who is ultimately 'alone onstage'. The question of mimesis is ambiguous in this solo piece for an actress. Is the Maid *imitating* various characters from her past and present such as the Mrs, the Uncle, the Priest, the Teacher and her younger self as the Niece? If so, then Maria demonstrates that she could have indeed been an actress, a notion she muses on in the play's final moments. Another approach is that each character is distinct from the Maid while the actual *actress* cast in this play transforms herself into multiple characters for the audience's sake. In this translation, we have worked from the assumption that Maria is impersonating the other characters since the playwright gives the distinct impression that this is a memory play. We also believe this is a more empowering interpretation of her character, since it shows how much Maria has retained and grown from the various people with whom she has interacted in life.

While playwright Mário Lúcio Sousa does not describe the geographical or temporal setting of the play, it seems clear from the original text that the action is set in the recent past in the Cape Verde Islands, West Africa. All other stage directions are translated from the playwright's original descriptions. Finally, we have heavily footnoted the translation to help the reader navigate through potentially unfamiliar references to Portuguese and Cape Verdean culture and history. – *Christina S. McMahon and Eunice S. Ferreira*

## NOTES

1. While this may seem like a typographical error, since it appears to be Maria speaking at the beginning of this passage, it actually functions as a reflexive self-interpellation by the playwright himself (Mário Lúcio Sousa). He seems to be infusing the start of the play with a set of questions for the reader to keep in mind as she or he navigates the more ambiguous, open-ended aspects of Maria's character. It is also interesting to think of Maria the character as a kind of gender-bending alter ego of the playwright

himself (although he occupies a much loftier social position and is highly educated, unlike his protagonist here). Mário Lúcio Sousa is the Minister of Culture in Cape Verde.

2. Sousa employs word-play here with a reference to Mariahilfe (a location that sounds like a woman's name) in Vienna, Austria.

3. Maria Callas was an American-born soprano (1923-1977) with a long opera career in Europe.

4. Bethânia (1946—), Brazilian singer and sister to the well-known singer and composer, Caetano Veloso.

5. Mary Pope Osborne (1949—) is a contemporary American children's book author.

6  Princess of Denmark and wife of the now deposed King Constantine II of Greece.

7. Walter de Maria (1935-2013) was an American sculptor and composer.

8. Latin for 'he said.'

9. For more on Cape Verdean emigration to São Tomé, see the accompanying article by McMahon in this issue.

10. The name given to this character in the original text is 'Mamãe Velha', a colloquial term that refers to a matriarchal figure such as a mother or grandmother. It is the opening address in the poem 'Regresso' ['Return'] by Amílcar Cabral, the leader of the joint liberation movement in Cape Verde and Guinea-Bissau. The poem also became a song famously recorded by Cesária Évora and Caetano Veloso. By opting for 'Auntie Nanny' in the English version, we are attempting to signify respect for an older woman without suggesting a blood relation, as is customary on the islands.

11. This line possibly refers to a trend among affluent Cape Verdeans to have a jacuzzi or sauna in their houses in order to keep their skin fresh and young-looking.

12. Sousa originally references Rosa Cant'ora, a known 'crazed woman' in Tarrafal on the main island of Santiago. 'Cantora' means singer in Portuguese.

13. Carlos Viegas Gago Coutinho was a Portuguese aviator who crossed the ocean on a seaplane from Lisbon to Rio de Janeiro in 1922, thus becoming the first person to traverse the South Atlantic Ocean by aircraft. While Gago is actually a part of his name, it also literally means 'stutterer' in Portuguese – hence Maria's amusement with all of the words in the book.

14. In the original text, the character describes himself as a 'seminarista', or seminarian. Here, 'seminary' probably refers to an elite academy for boys run by missionaries on São Nicolau Island in the late 19th and early 20th centuries. While some of the boys studied to be priests, others received formal education for the sake of later taking on civil service positions in the colonial government. Dessidério clearly opted for the second track, since he later became a Notary Public.

15. Both quotes in this passage come from Oscar Wilde's essay, 'The Decay of Lying – An Observation' (1891). See <http://www.online-literature.com/wilde/1307/> accessed 15 November 2013.

16. This line begins a series of quotations from Charles Baudelaire's poem, 'La Beauté', from his collection *Fleurs du mal* [*Flowers of Evil*], first published in 1857. We are drawing the English translations from *The Flowers of Evil,* trans. William Aggeler (Fresno, CA: Academic Library Guild, 1954), excerpted at <http://fleursdumal.org/poem/116> accessed 15 November 2013.

17. In Cape Verde's colonial education system, French was the second language taught (nowadays, Cape Verdean students can choose between studying French or English besides Portuguese). Both the French language and French literature were considered marks of high culture and prestige.

18. We have maintained the designation of lines to 'The Niece' here as in the original, but

Sousa's introduction of the dual designation of 'The Maid/The Niece' in the two lines of dialogue suggests a continual switching between the past and present. In performance, the Maid may shift in and out of her younger self as the Niece. Sousa imagines the reciting of Baudelaire, for example, as being done by an adolescent Maria. Another approach is that the Maid (Maria) is in the present moment attempting to conjure up the memory of her uncle by reciting his favorite poetry.

19. A passage from Charles Baudelaire's poem, 'Châtiment de l'Orgueil' ['Punishment for Pride'], from the same collection. We are again drawing the English translations from *The Flowers of Evil,* trans. William Aggeler (1954), excerpted at <http://fleurs dumal.org/poem/115> accessed 15 November 2013.

20. Ibid.

21. Another poem from Baudelaire's *Fleurs du mal* collection, this one called 'La Géante' ['The Giantess']. Once again, the English translation comes from *The Flowers of Evil,* trans. William Aggeler (Fresno, CA: Academic Library Guild, 1954), excerpted at: <http://fleursdumal.org/poem/118> accessed 19 November 2013.

22. This line is likely a veiled threat to get Dessidério sent to the Tarrafal Concentration Camp on Santiago Island in Cape Verde. Since Maria is 5 years old in this flashback, it takes place *circa* 1952. Between 1936 and 1954, Tarrafal was the prison to which the right-wing autocratic Salazar regime in Portugal sent those suspected of anti-fascist activities, including known communists. By then, French literature was probably regarded with more suspicion than it had been during the time Dessidério went to school as a young adult. In a later era, between 1961 and 1974, the Portuguese authorities re-opened the Tarrafal prison for Africans in its colonies who were suspected of anti-colonial activities.

23. Henri de Toulouse-Lautrec was a French Post-Impressionist painter whose art captured Parisian life in the late 1800s in all its decadence. He was also an alcoholic.

24. In the original Sousa specifies that she should be reciting swear words in Cape Verdean Crioulo, while the rest of the script, for the most part, is in Portuguese. He is likely producing this language shift in order to convey the raw emotion behind Maria's shock at seeing the images in the book.

25. In the original, the expression is 'nha mãe', which literally translates to 'my Mother' but corresponds to the English expression 'my God'. We have opted for the non-verbal expression 'Ai-yai-yai', since it is commonly used in Cape Verde (and other countries) to express surprise.

26. She is referring here to a cacau plantation on São Tomé, an island country that is a neighbor to Cape Verde. For more on Cape Verde's historical relationship to São Tomé, see the article by McMahon in this issue.

27. The port of Mindelo on the island of São Vicente has been an international nexus contributing to Mindelo's reputation as a 'cosmopolitan' city. The long-lasting influence of English coal merchants and other maritime traffic is evident in the traces of English in São Vicente Crioulo. Maria's reference to sighting Japanese men at the port reinforces the on-going significance of the commercial port to foreign investors.

28. 'Misses' references the popularity of various beauty pageants held in Cape Verde as well as international competitions such as the Miss Universe Pageant, which Maria seems to be watching on television. Cape Verdeans commonly call such pageants 'Miss', using the English word.

29. *Cachupa* is often celebrated as the national dish of Cape Verde. The homemade stew is a slow-boiled mix of hominy corn, beans, manioc, and fish or meat.

# Of Gender, Governance, and Goats: Locating Mário Lúcio Sousa's Unorthodox Drama in Cape Verdean Culture

## CHRISTINA S. McMAHON

In August 2009, Secretary of State Hillary Clinton made a whirlwind, seven-country African tour, her first major excursion to the continent as the newly appointed Secretary of State under the first Obama administration. Her inclusion of the Cape Verde Islands on that trip was puzzling. Global diplomatic tours are a matter of international strategy whether that means assessing prospects for financial investments or speaking out against social crises and government abuses of power (usually both, in the case of American diplomacy). These priorities were apparent in the majority of Clinton's destinations: Kenya, South Africa, Angola, Nigeria, the DRC. A set of ten tiny islands in West Africa with negligible natural resources and a solid record of peaceful government transitions since 1991 (when multi-party elections began), Cape Verde does not at first glance fit with the logic informing most of Clinton's other destinations. According to the Cape Verdean press, however, Clinton meant to hold up the archipelago to the rest of the continent as an example of good governance in Africa. The country's major news source, *A Semana* online, amply quoted Clinton's commendations of Cape Verde's political stability, economic growth, and gender parity in ministerial posts, seizing on this last point to emphasize that female empowerment was a driving impulse of Clinton's Africa tour (a point she made abundantly clear in a harsh rebuke to a Congolese student who had asked to hear her husband's political views).[1] By trumpeting Clinton's own refrain that Cape Verde should inspire other African governments to appoint more female leaders,[2] Cape Verdean media coverage of her visit unequivocally linked good governance to gender matters.

Certainly, gender does matter in the legal frameworks governing contemporary Cape Verdean society. At the time of Clinton's visit to the islands, Prime Minister José Maria Neves had just appointed three new women as government ministers, creating a majority female cabinet for the first time in Cape Verde's history.[3] Currently, the archipelago ranks among the top ten sub-Saharan African nations for strong female representation in government, with women occupying 20 per cent of Cape Verde's parliamentary seats.[4] Yet how do gender issues play out in the quotidian realm of household politics? Is the evolving balance of power in Cape Verdean government transferring to local family dynamics? Artists with keen eyes for gender issues can vividly bring these questions into public view, especially if they are writing for the stage. Such is the case with the dramatic oeuvre of Mário Lúcio Sousa, one of Cape Verde's best-known musicians and authors. Founder of the popular band, Simentera, and a successful solo artist, Sousa rounds out his remarkable talents with a substantial body of evocative poems and short stories, and a law degree to boot. In 2011, he was appointed Cape Verde's Minister of Culture.

Before attaining his high government position, Sousa wrote six plays that thoughtfully engaged with local Cape Verdean and African conundrums. Some of these have received prestigious stagings at Cape Verde's annual Mindelact International Theatre Festival and in performance venues throughout Portugal.[5] Lyrical, irreverent, and prolific (which is important within an emerging national theatre scene in Cape Verde where original, text-centred theatre often takes a back seat to adaptations of foreign works or improvisational comedies), Mário Lúcio Sousa is likely to be the playwright who puts Cape Verdean drama on the global map.

Sousa entered the theatre world in 2001, when he was commissioned to write a play about racism and social integration to be performed in Portugal's northern city of Porto, which had been named European Capital of Culture that year. The result was *Adão e as sete pretas de fuligem* [Adam and the Seven Soot-black Women], a satiric inversion of *Snow White and the Seven Dwarfs*. The play centres on Adão, a white *retornardo* of Portuguese descent, who is exiled to Portugal from the (unnamed) ex-African colony of his birth in the mid-1970s. This would have been just after the fall of the *Estado Novo*, the right-wing regime in Portugal that had been holding onto its African colonies with a death grip long after most other African nations had achieved independence. When Adão arrives in Lisbon, his experience with social exclusion eerily parallels that of six of the seven black African females of the title. They join him there, only to suffer from racism and sexism when they seek employment. Feeling acutely 'homeless', Adão makes rapid trips between Portugal and Africa yet finds cultural acceptance nowhere, since he feels too 'black' in Portugal and too 'white' in Africa. His path, as well as those of the *pretas*, redefines the diasporic lifestyle as locating solace in global circulation rather than any singular destination.[6]

Sousa accepted the challenge to write *Adão* at the behest of João Branco, a Portuguese theatre director working in Cape Verde and an admirer of Sousa's prose. Branco had secured an invitation to direct a new play for 'Porto 2001 – Capital Européia da Cultura'. Specifically, the programmers of the cultural festival had requested a Cape Verdean production to fill a slot in a performance cycle called 'Teatro dos Outros' [Theatre of Others]. While both playwright and director were wary of a category that explicitly 'othered' them alongside the Portuguese theatre on the programme,[7] they recognized a powerful opportunity to shed light on the racial exclusion experienced by Africans living in Portugal in the post-colonial era. Indeed, Branco reported that a large percentage of spectators who attended the five-day run of the show were Africans (mainly Cape Verdeans), many of them travelling to Porto from other cities such as Lisbon and Coimbra.[8]

The production later travelled to Rotterdam, a city that boasts a large Cape Verdean diaspora, and then returned to Cape Verde for the 2001 edition of the Mindelact International Theatre Festival, where it played on the main stage for 220 audience members consisting of Cape Verdean theatregoers living in the host city of Mindelo, Cape Verdean theatre artists who had travelled to Mindelo to perform at the festival, and visiting artists from Portugal, Spain, and Equatorial Guinea.[9] *Adão* was a highly anticipated production at Mindelact that year because of its recent European showings,[10] and it received a glowing review in a local newspaper for its enlightened portrayal of racism and homophobia.[11] The all-Cape Verdean cast utilized a primarily naturalistic acting style to portray their characters, and the production had a minimalist aesthetic – a series of black cubes transformed the space variously into street corners, cafés, and housing interiors – yet had a full lighting and sound design, as is standard for Mindelact productions. While the character of Adão wore white flowing clothes and a distinctly West African knitted Kufi hat (a costume design that could be interpreted as self-exoticism in response to the Porto festival committee's original desire to see an African 'other' onstage),[12] the six female stars wore solid-coloured dresses in different hues that created a rainbow-like effect when they were all together in a scene.

The woman-centred cast of *Adão e as sete pretas de fuligem* meshed well with João Branco's penchant for directing plays that explore female psyches and Cape Verdean women's social predicaments. Yet I am far from suggesting here that Mário Lúcio Sousa can be considered a feminist playwright. In fact, *Adão e as sete pretas de fuligem* turns upon many plot points that would have feminist readers up in arms. When the protagonist proposes that his female friends move with him to his family's house in Porto, where they will 'bring Africa to Portugal' by cooking their native food, dressing in African attire, and working communally, seemingly innocuous diasporic desires are unveiled as mere pretence for white male colonization of black women's bodies.[13] Put simply, Adão proposes to be a 'traditional African chief' who reserves the final word on all household decisions, and demands visitation rights to the women's beds: 'Aqui todos me obedecem' [Here, everyone obeys me].[14] Adão's nocturnal sojourn in the house is ultimately blocked by a series of Christian saints who confront him (portrayed by marionettes in Branco's production), ostensibly in an effort to protect the women's bodies from his exploitative desires. Yet the play as a whole lacks the ironic narrative distance that might raise serious questions about the protagonist's womanizing proclivities; in this case, a form of household governance in a supposedly communal house that Adão identifies as 'African' is simply a self-serving masculinist fantasy about Africa.

Nevertheless, Cape Verde's storehouse of national drama cannot help but be enriched by a playwright who trades in gender politics and dabbles in queer issues, a bold move in a country wherein *machismo* reigns and homosexuality remains a social taboo.[15] In *Adão,* a queer-identified Portuguese black man, Preta (the seventh *preta* of the play's title), voices the passage that packs the play's most searing socio-political punch: 'Porque o mudo tem língua, mas não fala. Há-os também que têm língua e fala, mas não têm voz. Alguns ainda têm língua, voz e fala, mas não são ouvidos, Adão' [Because the mute has a tongue, but doesn't speak. There are also those who have a tongue and speak, but don't have a voice. Still others have a tongue, voice, and speak, but aren't heard, Adam].[16] The characters in Sousa's plays are examples of this marginalization; they are people who, for numerous reasons, must strain to make their muted voices heard in their societies. In most cases, these characters are women.

*Salon,* Sousa's second play, provides a good example. The protagonist is a deaf (lip-reading) hairstylist who has to constantly remind people that her deafness does not make her voiceless as well: 'Surda, surda, sim! Mas, muda não! Eu posso falar' [Yes, yes I'm deaf! But not mute. I can speak] (p. 86). Cabaleireira (whose name means hairdresser in Portuguese) has a childhood friend named Fofó who convinces her to open a salon where the two of them can eavesdrop on clients, thus gaining access to their community's most coveted secrets, scandalous gossip, and political intrigue. Fofó reasons that a salon with a deaf stylist will be irresistible to women longing to speak without being 'heard'. How, then, to capture the juicy tidbits? Enter Tulipa, the hairdresser's billy goat. Fofó decrees that the odorous Tulipa be tied to a post adjacent to a styling-chair far from where she herself will be concealed in a barrel, poised to overhear clients. When they enter the salon, the stylist must inquire: 'A senhora deseja tratamento de estética simples ou com cheiro a bode? Com cheiro a bode é mais caro' [Does madam want the simple aesthetic treatment, or with the scent of a goat? The goat's scent costs more] (p. 83). Fofó reasons that most women will choose the chair closest to the barrel (and her listening ears), fleeing both the goat's smell and the higher rates. The absurd plan, of course, is foolproof.

*Salon* was well-received when it debuted in 2002 at the Mindelact festival for an audience of Cape Verdean nationals as well as visiting artists from Portugal, Brazil, Guinea-Bissau, Senegal, and Guinea Equatorial. The all-female cast sported artistic hairstyles with loops, braids, and vibrant colours that reflected the lighthearted spirit of the show. While the set was semi-naturalistic – a hair salon constructed mainly from large plastic canisters – the story's bizarre premise dipped further into absurdism than Sousa's previous work. Sousa playfully alluded to this when he described his second play as Ab Surda (*surda* is the Portuguese word for deaf).[17] Yet his brand of dramaturgy cannot be confused with the more familiar rubric of 'Theatre of the Absurd'. Celebrated absurdist playwrights from theatre history, such as Samuel Beckett and Eugène Ionesco, show us a world steeped in irrationality, which only intensifies as its human inhabitants hunt for order within it; Sousa's plays begin nonsensically but conclude with a return to normalcy that implies that twists of logic, rather than paradox, govern human lives. In *Salon,* Fofó's machinations uncover a wildly improbable amorous saga pieced together from a string of motley clients: a street fish-seller who bellows to passers-by in Crioulo, Cape Verde's local language; a stuttering hippie girl who alters her hair colour daily; a Bible-wielding holy roller; a gold-draped, freshly returned emigrant with a thick Italian accent; and a placid high-society woman married to a government minister.

The surprise is that the government official, Benjamin, is ex-lover to nearly all the women who breeze through the salon that day, including Cabaleireira and Fofó. Climbing the social/sexual ladder with aplomb, he has wrung resources from each of the women, metamorphosing from full-time loafer to municipal gravedigger, to co-owner of a funeral salon,

*Figure 1: The cast of* Adão e as sete pretas de fuligem *in a production performed as part of the festivities for 'Porto 2001 – Capital Européia da Cultura' in Portugal. Photo by Henrique Delgado, courtesy of the Mindelact Association.*

*Figure 2: The cast of* Salon *in a production by GTCCPM (Grupo de Teatro do Centro Cultural Português do Mindelo) for the 2002 Mindelact International Theatre Festival in Cape Verde. Photo by João Branco, courtesy of the Mindelact Association.*

*Figure 3: Ana Perfeito and Patrícia Esteves in a production of* Sozinha no Palco *by the company Teatro Reactor performed for the 2007 Mindelact International Theatre Festival in Cape Verde Verde. Photo by João Barbosa, courtesy of the Mindelact Association.*

emigrant to Europe, doctoral student in the USA, and finally Ministro de Ordenamento do Território [Minister of Territorial Ordering] in Cape Verde. Benjamin is the polar opposite of the kind of government minister Hillary Clinton extolled in 2009. Not only is he male, he is an exploiter of women.

Mário Lúcio Sousa once said in an interview that he considers hair salons to be the most democratic locales in Cape Verde. Inside, everyone has the right to speak and invent that which one does not know.[18] This conviction is evident in *Salon*. Unlike *Adão e as sete pretas de fuligem*, the philanderer is conspicuously absent in this play. This grants the female characters space to vent their frustration with the *machismo* they have suffered and converse about the vicissitudes of their lives. All exercise a voice; all demonstrate personal resilience. As the play unfolds, the utility of Tulipa the billy goat disappears. By the last scene, Fofó has emerged from the barrel and the women dialogue openly about their pasts. Significantly, the Portuguese word for billy goat that Sousa uses is *bode*, which can also be slang for 'problem', 'bad experience', or 'scapegoat'. In the play, Benjamin becomes all of these things to the various women. He is their *bode*, and, like Tulipa, he loses ultimately his functionality when the women realize they no longer need him to make sense of their lives. This is a different kind of female empowerment from that which Clinton lauded, surely, but empowerment nonetheless.

Clinton's commendations of gender parity on the islands remained on the macro level, relating to women who occupy the highest national posts. But governance operates most stealthily on the micro level, in the day-to-day struggles Cape Verdean women face: limited access to employment and education, unequal pay, inadequate childcare, and inheritance disputes, which are prevalent in a country where one man might sustain households with a number of different women. A poll that *A Semana* online conducted in 2005 asked, 'Are Cape Verdean women emancipated?' Most respondents indicated that, despite provisions for their rights in the constitution, many Cape Verdean women still have not obtained economic independence or juridical protection.[19] This is particularly true of poor women who lack formal education and access to professional career opportunities. Such women fly beneath the radar of the 'good governance' so often touted in Cape Verde. And it is precisely these kinds of women that Mário Lúcio Sousa's theatre allows Cape Verdean spectators to glimpse and critically ponder upon.

Such an opportunity arose five years later at the 2007 Mindelact International Theatre Festival, when the Portuguese theatre troupe, Teatro

Reactor, debuted *Sozinha no palco* [Alone Onstage] which Sousa wrote in 2003 as a solo piece for an actress – its appearance in this issue of *Moving Worlds* marks the first English translation of a play by Sousa. Set in the recent past, *Sozinha no palco* whisks through an indigent domestic servant's first day working for a wealthy Cape Verdean family with the ideologically loaded surname of Império [Empire]. Maria (a name that suggests a kind of Cape Verdean 'everywoman') is illiterate but is paradoxically obsessed with books. Her musings on Baudelaire (whom her pedantic uncle and guardian quoted liberally when she was a child) and the Kama Sutra (which she discovers on Mr Empire's bookshelf) drift haphazardly into her poignant memories of relocating as a young woman to the island country of São Tomé, home of the cacao plantations that figure nightmarishly in Cape Verde's history of forced labour migration under Portuguese colonialism.

*Sozinha no palco* examines how divergent social positions and educational trajectories have shaped the destinies of various Cape Verdean subjects in the colonial and post-independence eras. Maria's uncle, Dessidério, identifies himself as a 'seminarian'. Given his age and birthplace, Dessidério was probably a graduate of the *Seminário-Liceu*, a secondary school on São Nicolau Island that missionaries ran in the late nineteenth and early twentieth centuries for young men who aspired either to the priesthood or a civil service career with the colonial government. At this elite school, students acquired knowledge of European literature and culture, as well as a firm command of the Portuguese language, which were exactly the requirements for attaining *assimilado* ['assimilated'] status in the Portuguese colonial system. Dessidério certainly achieved this elevated standing since he later became a Notary Public. While *assimilados* could access many of the same citizenship rights as Portuguese nationals, including the right to vote, Cape Verdeans classified as *indigenatos* (normally poor, illiterate people in rural areas) could not, and were subject to labour conscription during tough economic times.[20] While the colonial government in Cape Verde officially abolished the *indigenato* laws in 1947, which would have been six years before Maria's birth, destitute islanders were, in practice, still dehumanized by authorities and excluded from the privileges of citizenship. During periods of severe drought on the islands, many Cape Verdean labourers had little choice but to pursue exploitative work contracts in São Tomé.[21] This is probably what happened to Maria, a poor relation of her *assimilado* uncle, in the years after his death.

In *Sozinha no palco*, Maria openly announces that she does not have a voice, and therefore does not need to have opinions. Yet in the course of the play, Maria expounds on a variety of topics, from nuclear testing grounds to the ludicrous extravagance of the wealthy classes. Through her uncanny imitations of her uncle, a priest, her primary school teacher, and Mrs Empire, Maria demonstrates her sponge-like capacity to absorb knowledge and transform it into her own unique perspective on life. Thus she calls into question the presumed hierarchy of book learning over innate intelligence, even offering pearls of folk wisdom gleaned from her years labouring in São Tomé, a place long regarded as a cultural and epistemological void from the perspective of the colonial authorities and the upper classes in Cape Verde. What ultimately empowers Maria is the richness of her own memories, her wide-ranging sensibility, and a keen self-awareness lacking in her employers. While this by no means evens the playing field between Maria and Mrs Empire (who would have fitted the category of 'assimilated' in colonial times), the play at least demonstrates how women like Maria may share in the kind of knowledge production normally associated solely with those of a higher class and social position in Cape Verde.

Yet the play's postcolonial implications were difficult to access in the 2007 Teatro Reactor production. Brazilian director, William Gavião, opted for an overtly over-the-top performance style, employing two white Portuguese actresses dressed identically in billowing cream dresses and absurdist birdlike masks to portray the various characters Maria embodies. The minimalist set consisted of two wooden planks that variously served as podiums for the actresses' speeches (delivered in an exaggerated manner) and the two doors in the house through which characters constantly enter and exit. In some ways, this farcical performance style makes sense for a play that explicitly references Oscar Wilde, and Sousa himself told me that he admired the imaginative interpretation that Gavião brought to the text.[22] However, as a spectator at Mindelact 2007, I did feel a tinge of disappointment that the production failed to engage the play's racial implications and its exploration of colonial legacies. Indeed, the casting of two actresses in the play meant that the scene with the primary school teacher, as well as the ones with Uncle Dessidério, ended up replicating the very knowledge binaries that Sousa's text so powerfully challenges, since Maria became a student kneeling at these other characters' feet rather than an agential impersonator of them. The actresses also played the Kama Sutra scene – where Maria starts trying out the unusual sexual positions with her own body – purely for laughs, sashaying around the stage with veils while Indian music played in the background and then acting out the positions with each other in a slapstick manner. In the text, this scene does come across as humorous. Yet it also has a larger meaning that was lost in the production, which is that Maria's quest for knowledge is here deeply embodied. Despite not being able to read the large book, she is able to explore new ideas and philosophies in a corporeal manner which is certainly an empowering way of being in the world.

Teatro Reactor's production did have certain clear advantages: to my knowledge, it was the first occasion a visiting theatre company performed an original play by a Cape Verdean author at Mindelact, a homage in other words to the flourishing theatre scene on the islands. Further, the director and actresses managed to develop a highly original concept for the *mise en scène* previously unfathomable to those who had read the text,[23] proving that Sousa's writing has a kind of elasticity that facilitates border-crossing and invokes new cultural interpretations. The major disadvantage was the inflated acting style and the casting of white Portuguese actresses. This meant that the production glided over the institutionalized racism and classism that had led to compulsory or economically propelled migration during Maria's lifetime. As a result, the lines about São Tomé rang hollow during the production. This is perhaps an argument for increasing the circulation of Cape Verdean plays, since theatre groups from, say, São Tomé, Angola, or the Caribbean might be more inclined to highlight the postcolonial nuances of *Sozinha no palco*. Teatro Reactor's production did, however, successfully capture the bittersweet final reflections of this unlettered woman who, as we learn, has always dreamed of occupying a spotlight onstage, but never in a solo production:

> Se eu soubesse escrever era isso que eu escreveria. O meu primeiro dia como empregada doméstica. Não pelo que eu fiz nesse dia, mas pelo que eu não fiz. Pois, não me quis ver sozinha num palco.
> [If I knew how to write, this is what I would have written about: My first day as a maid. Not for what I did on this day, but for what I did not do. All because I did not want to see myself alone onstage.] (p. 196)

I vividly recall the sharp intake of breath that arose from the Mindelact audience at the actress's affecting final words, delivered in silhouette: 'Agora, eis-me aqui, sozinha na vida. Sozinha, com as minhas lembranças' [And now here I am, alone in life. Alone, with my memories] (p. 196).

While *Sozinha no palco* adopts the medium of introspective dreamscape, a more recent Sousa play injects political parody into the exploration of gender and governance. Boasting a title sustained upon contradictions,

*24 Horas na vida de um morto* [24 Hours in the Life of a Dead Man] revolves around the farcical situation of a deceased person who, in his will, bequeaths his hand in marriage to his long-time domestic partner, who has helped to raise his child by another woman. Sousa wrote the play in 2005 specifically to be performed by the graduating class of an introductory theatre course that Cape Verdean actor, João Paulo Brito, had led that year in Praia, Cape Verde's capital city, and the place where Sousa currently lives, on the southern island of Santiago. In an interview, Sousa once explained to me that writing theatre for Santiago actors requires a unique approach that captures the spontaneity, rhythm, and profound investment in tradition that exemplifies the cultural landscape of Cape Verde's most populous island.[24] *24 Horas na vida de um morto* afforded Sousa the chance to capture the idiosyncrasies of life on his home island. The play debuted at the Portuguese Cultural Center (CCP) in Praia in 2006 with Brito directing. A reviewer for a local newspaper commended the Praia production for its inventive scenic design (for example, a series of simple mats hanging from the ceiling to indicate doors, rather than the naturalistic approach to scenery often adopted in Praia theatre) and its unusual interpretation of mourning rituals on Santiago Island (Sousa specifies in the written text that no 'crying scenes' may take place in productions of the play, presumably so that actors would not fall into stereotypes of grieving rituals and would focus more on the political parody).[25]

In the play, the dead man's unusual deposition sparks uproar in his community. While his young nephew and domestic partner move fervently ahead with the funeral-wedding plans (with the latter commissioning a tailor to stitch her black widow's weeds as well as a white wedding dress), his daughter chastens her for inappropriately scheming to marry her deceased father. Meanwhile, two competing political factions, called simply 'Party A' and 'Party B,' debate how each can spin death to its own advantage by taking a strategic stance on the issue of 'marriage by last will and testimony'. In a swipe presumably at Cape Verde's two major parties, the PAICV (African Party for the Independence of Cape Verde) and the MpD (Movement for Democracy), Party A and Party B are nearly indistinguishable in their rhetoric, the two leaders' opening addresses to their respective parties differing only in one instance when Leader B inserts the word 'opposition' before 'party'.

Seemingly, the play operates as a biting commentary on the impotence of Cape Verdean women in the face of state law, not as it is penned in the constitution but as it plays out in everyday life. As one woman in the community quips, allowing the widow of a common law marriage to marry her deceased partner legally is proof positive that Cape Verde is a 'democracy'. Another woman chimes in with, 'Sorte grande! Casar-se com o marido já com pé na cova. Com o divórcio já dado, com a separação já consumada, com o reencontro já marcado no céu' [What luck! Marrying a man with one foot already in the grave. With divorce already a given, separation already consummated, and the reunion already scheduled in heaven] (p. 154). In this utopian vision, a Cape Verdean widow can access all of the privileges of marriage (inheritance, property, legitimacy in the eyes of her community) without the accompanying inconveniences of an actual union: patriarchal household governance, polygyny, and the underlying threat of domestic violence.[26]

While the community's women are left to comment on the predicament in hushed tones among themselves in the parlour, party members occupy the overtly political terrain of a governmental campaign promising the actual legislative power to make changes to Cape Verde's constitution. Assuming that the party members are all male (Sousa gives them only generic names like 'Fanatic A' and 'Militant B'), this spatial divide could represent a schism of the private and public spheres along gender lines: a situation that would be wide open for critique from discerning Cape Verdean theatre audiences. Strikingly, the way in which a theatre director chooses to cast the political party members (as all men, all women, or a mix) would determine how gender parity plays out both onstage and within the fictional legal realm depicted in *24 Horas*.

In *24 Horas*, the resolution is nearly as absurd as its premise. The feuding family calls in the neighbourhood *dodu* [crazy man], who had transcribed the will for the deceased. When asked to explain the testimony's cryptic line, he voices two theories of transcription: 'Ou escrevemos exactamente aquilo que ouvimos. Ou escrevemos aquilo que pensamos que as pessoas quiseram dizer' [Either we write exactly what we hear, or we write what we think people wanted to say] (p. 174). Having explained that he chose the former route, and that, revealingly, the deceased was a cleft-lipped man whose speech was often jumbled, the *dodu* discloses that the dead man actually meant to leave his *património* [patrimony, or estate] to his widow, rather than his *matrimónio* [marriage]. Here, we have an interesting twist on the insight provided by the character of Preta in Sousa's first play, *Adão*. Even though the cleft-lipped man had a voice but was not heard (or at least transcribed) accurately, his domestic partner, a character with even less social standing, still benefits. Although she loses out on the privileges of marriage, she gains what has probably been her ulterior motive in seeking a legal union with a dead man in the first place: his land.

*24 Horas* is a play meticulously concerned with alphabets and grammar. This occurs even at the level of dialogue, most of which is written in Cape Verdean Crioulo, a mixture of archaic Portuguese and various West African languages. As this was Sousa's first attempt to write drama in Crioulo, a language that lacks a stable standardized form, any pages of the text include painstakingly written footnotes explaining pronunciations of phonemes nonexistent in Portuguese, such as 'Tx' (tch), or detailing the divergent intonations given to a single vowel sound on Cape Verde's various islands (such as 'A'). In some ways, the whole play is a literacy lesson in Cape Verdean Crioulo for readers of Portuguese, with Sousa acting as the patient teacher. Readers will certainly struggle, as did my Mozambican friend, actress Graça da Silva, who professed enormous frustration in trying to decode the Crioulo dialogue in the play. Cape Verdeans themselves are unaccustomed to reading texts in Crioulo; Portuguese forms the bedrock of the written word in Cape Verde.

Yet this tricky linguistic exercise may make readers more empathetic to the plight of the rural, unschooled characters at the heart of the play. Readers struggling to interpret Crioulo mirror the protagonists' inability to read and write Portuguese. The dead man, for instance, had to rely on the local madman to write his will with ludicrous results. The play therefore illustrates how the gates of illiteracy too often shut out poor and rural populations from the world of meaning that surrounds them. Across the archipelago, illiteracy rates are considerably higher among women than men, owing chiefly to the tendency among rural families to keep daughters at home to help with chores. *24 Horas* demonstrates how drastically such a scenario might impact on women's life chances: the dead man's partner ceded power over her own destiny because she needed to rely on her nephew and neighbours to interpret her husband's will for her. Lacking the ability to read, she could only be a reactor to the news conveyed to her by literate friends. The play thus shows the flip side of the 'empowerment' Clinton spied in Cape Verdean female government ministers by foregrounding the illiterate, rural woman who must labour just to govern her own life.

Mário Lúcio Sousa's theatre, with its unorthodox rules and implausible plots, forces us to see disempowered women with fresh eyes and from novel perspectives. His placement of them at the centre of his drama also opens up new opportunities for Cape Verdean actresses to perform challenging roles – a crucial condition in a local theatre scene in which male actors dominate, since young women's families or partners may discourage them from attending rehearsals or performing at all.[27] Yet Sousa's theatre need no longer be restricted to Cape Verde. In recent years, the Mindelact Theatre Association has taken the vital initiative of publishing drama anthologies by emerging Cape Verdean playwrights. This enables Cape Verdean dramaturgy to reach new theatre audiences (my Mozambican friend, Graça da Silva, told me she wishes to one day play Maria in a production of *Sozinha no palco*) and new readerships (without my now well-worn copy of *Mário Lúcio Sousa: Teatro* [2008] by my side, I could not have written this article).

In an illuminating 'offstage voice' passage that serves as a prelude to *Sozinha no palco*, Sousa himself seems to grapple with the complicated implications of his unique female characters. Even though the play seemingly begins from the viewpoint of Maria (since the stage directions mention the silhouette of a woman and the dialogue references a person who identifies herself as illiterate), the speaker inexplicably switches mid-stream to the voice of the playwright himself, who re-creates a (fictional?) letter addressed to him from his uncle:

Olá Mário, tudo bem? Já li e reli a peça e não percebi qual é a linha de força, o que queres contar. ...Acho as personagens pouca claras e não sei qual é a função delas. ... Gostaria que se tivesses tempo trabalhasses mais o texto. O que a mulher tem de especial para que a história dela mereça ser contada e principalmente ouvida? Qual é o conflito dela? O que deixará de si nas pessoas que a escutam? (p. 181)[28]

A brilliantly self-reflexive overture to a play that offers no easy solutions to gender dilemmas in Cape Verde, the passage also invites readers, actors, directors, scholars, and potential translators to wrestle with the appropriate interpretive stances to adopt towards Maria and the multitudes of unsung heroines she represents.

> Hey Mário, how's it going? I read and re-read the play and I don't understand its line of action, what story you want to tell. ... I find the characters unclear and I don't understand their function. ... I wish you had more time to work on the text. *What makes the woman so special that her story deserves to be told, and principally, heard? What's her conflict? What will she leave behind in the people who listen to her?*

## NOTES

This article benefited greatly from careful feedback provided by Jeff Hessney, to whom I am most grateful.

1. Specifically, the student asked about Mr Clinton's opinion of Chinese investment in the Congo, to which Hillary Clinton sharply retorted that she was Secretary of State, not her husband. After the incident made worldwide news, Clinton publicly apologised for her curt response, while the student explained that he had meant to say

'Mr. Obama'. See Jeffrey Gettleman, 'Clinton's Flash of Peak in the Congo', *New York Times*, 13 August 2009, <http://www.nytimes.com/2009/08/13/world/africa/13 clinton.html?_r=0> accessed 25 October 2013.

2. 'Hillary Clinton departs from Cape Verde enchanted', *A Semana* online, 15 August 2009, <www.asemana.publ.cv/spip.php?article44489&var_recherche=hillary%20clin ton&ak=1> accessed 16 August 2009.

3. See 'Profunda Remodelação Governmental em Cabo Verde', <http://www.panapress. com/Profunda-remodelacao-governamental-em-Cabo-Verde—12-427198-96-lang1-index.html> accessed 27 November 2013.

4. See 'Women in Parliaments: World Classifications', <http://www.ipu.org/wmn-e/classif.htm> accessed 25 October 2013.

5. Sousa's seventh play, *Adão e Eva* [Adam and Eve], recently debuted at the 2013 Mindelact International Theatre Festival in Cape Verde in a production directed by João Paulo Brito.

6. See Christina S. McMahon, 'Embodying Diaspora: Ambivalence and Utopia in Contemporary Cape Verdean Theatre', *Theatre History Studies*, 27 (2007) 110-38.

7. In a short article published in the Mindelact Association's cultural magazine, Branco lamented that their production was pigeonholed into the category of 'African theatre', when what they actually wanted to produce was 'theatre', a story recognized as valid in any cultural context. João Branco, 'A visão do encenador', *Mindelact: Teatro em revista*, 9 (2001) 14-17.

8. Ibid.

9. Since Mindelact is a fairly small-scale international theatre festival, performances typically run for one night only. The main venue, the Mindelo Cultural Centre, has a capacity of 220, so the debut of *Adão e as sete pretas de fuligem* did play to a full house.

10. João Almeida, 'Gloriosa passagem pela Europa', *A Semana*, 13 July 2001.

11. João Almeida, 'Mindelact 2001: Espectáculos de tirar o fôlego', *A Semana*, 21 September 2001.

12. My thanks to Eunice Ferreira for suggesting this insight in a conversation we had about the production.

13. However, the racial implications of this scene were probably clouded in the production, since it was actually a Cape Verdean actor, João Brito, who played Adão, a character scripted as a white Portuguese man born in Africa. While Brito is light-skinned, he is visibly as Cape Verdean as the rest of the cast. Therefore, what audiences saw onstage was a Cape Verdean actor playing a *machista* character, which potentially reinforced problematic stereotypes of African masculinity and sexuality.

14. All translations of excerpts from Sousa's plays are my own. The exception is *Sozinha no palco*, for which I am quoting passages from the translation published in this issue by Eunice Ferreira and myself.

15. A new gay rights organization in Cape Verde signals a more vocal public outcry against these social norms. In 2012, a group of young people living in Mindelo and identifying as gay, bisexual, and transgender formed a new NGO called Associação Gay Cabo-verdiana contra a Discriminação [Cape Verdean Gay Association against Discrimination]. This group has been partnering with more established NGOs in the country to raise awareness about issues such as targeted street violence against sexual minorities. See Susana Rendall Rocha, 'Mindelo: Gays, lésbicas e simpatizantes em oficina de saúde sexual 12 Outubro 2012', *A Semana Online*, 12 October 2012, <http://asemana.publ.cv/spip.php?article81023&ak=1> accessed 22 March 2013.

16. Mário Lúcio Sousa, *Teatro* (Mindelo,:Cape Verde: The Mindelact Association, 2008), p. 41. All further page references are to this edition and are included in the text of the

article.

17. Mário Lúcio Sousa, 'Salon, uma casa Ab Surda', *Mindelact: Teatro em revista*, 11 (2002) 24.

18. Fonseca Soares, 'Entrevista com Mário Lúcio', *Mindelact: Teatro em revista*, 9 (2001) 18-22.

19. 'A mulher cabo-verdiana é emancipada?,' *A Semana* online, (8 March 2005), <www.asemana.cv/article.php3?id_article=10481&langue=CV> accessed 11 March 2008.

20. See Kesha Fikes, 'Emigration and the Spatial Production of Difference in Cape Verde', in *Race and Globalization: Transformations in the Cultural Production of Blackness*, ed. by Kamari Maxine Clarke and Deborah A. Thomas (Durham, NC: Duke UP, 2006), pp. 154-70.

21. See Augusto Nascimento, 'Cape Verdeans in São Tomé and Princípe', in *Transnational Archipelago: Perspectives on Cape Verdean Migration and Diaspora*, ed. by Luís Batalha and Jørgen Carling (Amsterdam: Amsterdam University Press, 2008), pp. 55-60.

22. Mário Lúcio Sousa, email to the author, 24 April 2009.

23. After the 2007 production, I conducted a spectator interview with João Paulo Brito, the same actor who had created the role of Adão in Sousa's first play. Brito had read *Sozinha no palco* when it was published in an edition of *Mindelact: Teatro em revista* devoted to new Cape Verdean plays (vol. 12-13, 2003). Like Sousa, Brito was completely in favour of Teatro Reactor's interpretation, declaring that it successfully married the text's local references with its more global-reaching themes. João Paulo Brito, interview with the author, 13 September 2007.

24. Mário Lúcio Sousa, interview with the author, 8 September 2005.

25. PMC, '"24 Horas na nida de um morto" ao ritmo da Praia', *A Semana*, 24 February 2006.

26. For more on how these issues play out in the lives of Cape Verdean women, see Marla Jill Solomon, '"We Can Even Feel that We are Poor, but We Have a Strong and Rich Spirit": Learning from the Lives and Organization of the Women of Tira Chapeu, Cape Verde' (unpublished doctoral thesis, University of Massachusetts, 1992); and Katherine Carter and Judy Aulette, *Cape Verdean Women and Globalization: The Politics of Gender, Culture, and Resistance* (New York: Palgrave Macmillan, 2009).

27. This is something I heard often from the actresses and female dancers I interviewed during my fieldwork trips to Cape Verde from 2004 to 2007.

28. Teatro Reactor cut this passage in its production, presumably because the company found it confusing or thought the audience would.

# 'Contemporary Dance, not African Dance': The Question of a Contemporary Nigerian Dance

## CHUKWUMA OKOYE

### Introduction

In a post-performance talk at The Place in London on 10 November 2004, Adedayo Liadi, a leading Nigerian dancer/choreographer, was asked why his company, Ijodee Dance Company, did not perform in African costumes. He stated that his dance was not 'African dance' but 'Contemporary dance'.[1] While his interrogator evoked that stereotypical perception of African identity as Europe's Other – a vision of African dance as comprising feral tribesmen clad in raffia skirts stomping about in wild ecstasy to the entrancing rhythm of ecstatic drumming – Liadi's riposte is a strong rebuttal of that cultural stereotyping in which to be authentic the African artist must stay within the walls of 'tradition' and not attempt, like Liadi, to wander into the world of modernity. As Olu Oguibe aptly observes:

> The issue of authenticity and its attendant anxieties are of course not matters over which contemporary African artists are likely to be found losing any sleep. On the contrary, it is those who construct authenticities and fabricate identities for them who are constantly plagued with worries. ... such anxieties have less to do with facts of authenticity and the relevance of tradition, as with a desire to force African artists behind the confines of manufactured identities aimed to place a distance between their practice and the purloined identity of contemporary Caucasian art. In other words, the introduction of the question of authenticity is only a demand for identity, a demand for the signs of difference, a demand for cultural distance.[2]

Evidently, Liadi is not the only contemporary artist rejecting this sign of difference. Regarding the reception of contemporary African film in Europe, Olivier Barlet identifies a mode of reception which decries any attempt to deviate from that romantic image of Africa that French critics relish.

> This attitude takes the form of a stunning ignorance of the existence of contemporary art in those countries, and the rejection of any autonomous expression which does not correspond to Western 'exotic' expectations ... It is in order to sidestep this demand for cultural difference, which slips surreptitiously into film criticism, that young directors living in Europe reject the term 'African filmmaker' with vigour.[3]

This exoticization of African art by European audiences is no different from the manner in which some Nigerian elites receive contemporary dance in Nigeria.[4] There is a band of self-appointed defenders of 'our culture' who finds it impossible to imagine authenticity as anything but hermetic, and contemporaneity as anything other than cultural betrayal and the triumph of Western cultural hegemony. Unfortunately, these defenders of our cultural universe are informed Nigerians who conduct their businesses safely ensconced within the walls constructed not by 'authentic' Africa but by that very culture of 'imperialism'. I have witnessed a Professor of Theatre Arts in Nigeria affirm, quite dismissively, that there is nothing original or authentic in Adedayo Liadi's choreography. He claimed that Liadi was simply promoting Western culture at the expense of his own indigenous Yoruba heritage. He challenged the already intimidated student who had dared to write a dissertation on contemporary Nigerian dance to state what was precisely Nigerian in any of Liadi's performances. Ironically, this harassment was conducted in the English language and the Professor is a 'distinguished scholar' in an institution that is not designed after his authentic Nigerian prototype. My 'authentic' ancestors prized knowledge so highly that an Igbo proverb avers that the person who travels the most is often the most knowledgeable because he acquires knowledge from everywhere and returns home to nourish the existing fount of communal wisdom. My ancestors were quite critical of the category they conceived of as intellectual geckos who do not wander beyond the walls of the homestead, but stay at home only to drain the familial stock. Thus my ancestors, who constructed those systems of intellectual and embodied knowledge that make up the Igbo tradition, never questioned any cultural import on the basis of its origin but only of its usefulness.

However, this desire for Africa's authenticity has not really arisen out of ignorance, especially as evidenced in the Professor's case. Indeed there is a structural correlation between the lust for authenticity and knowledge: the desire for authenticity is the result of a feeling of estrangement in scholars who are already steeped in Western knowledge. According to Erik Cohen,

> Alienation and the quest for authenticity … appear to be positively related. It follows that intellectuals and other more alienated individuals will engage on a more serious quest of authenticity than most rank-and-file members of society. It is hypothesized further that, the greater their concern for authenticity, the stricter will be the criteria by which they conceive of it.[5]

In this paper I investigate the contentious status of contemporary dance in Nigeria. Taking Adedayo Liadi's work as my critical lodestar, I examine the charge of cultural saboteur against practitioners of contemporary Nigerian dance. I hope to demonstrate that there certainly is a dance form that can definitively be described as contemporary Nigerian dance. And to reveal in Liadi's choreographic enterprise a fusion of his indigenous culture, his training in Euro-American dance, and his contemporary socio-cultural life experience into a refreshing expression that is at once personal and communal, novel as well as familiar. I argue that contemporary Nigerian dance is a spatially and rhythmically embodied creative and dynamic category that challenges received orthodoxies – in both the indigenous Nigerian and Western aesthetic configurations – and critiques the complex peculiarities and vicissitudes of daily living in contemporary Nigeria.

## Contemporary dance

Dance has been notoriously marginalized, especially in scholarly investigations of the arts in Nigeria. The irony is that in practice dance is easily the most ubiquitous performance form in our daily living. A number of factors can be held accountable for the sorry state of dance scholarship in Nigeria. First, very few scholars are trained in dance appreciation. Second, the nature of dance itself, its ephemeral character, makes it impossible to capture or arrest performances for close analysis, except through film/video recording. Third, because it is a non-verbal medium, dance is difficult to describe or analyse. Thus, in the academy where textuality and logocentrism hold sway, dance presents a problem not many scholars are anxious to confront: it cannot easily be 'read' because it does not always embody literal messages and narratives. Because of these difficulties the few scholarly investigations of the phenomenon have been mostly concerned with its social functions, neglecting its formal status as a work of art.[6] Failure to examine dance as an aesthetic expression of body movements is, according to Roderyk Lange, clearly inapt: 'The description of impressions ... gained when viewing dance, may certainly be an important source of information. However, it amounts to talking about or around a dance rather than truly *describing* it.'[7]

This difficulty in dance criticism becomes even more acute in the case of contemporary dance, a problem rendered virtually intractable by the very complexity and arbitrariness of the new form, such as its virtual resistance to description due to its formal instability, its programmatic departure from pre-existing dance styles while refusing to take any definitive form itself, and its sheer valorization of creative freedom.

As a formal artistic category, contemporary dance has a rather nebulous origin. Although the field did not come to be so named until the 1980s, the various techniques and ideologies that eventually melded to constitute the genre can be traced to a more distant past, to the United States in the 1950s, and such pioneer dancers/choreographers as Martha Graham, Merce Cunningham, and Lester Horton. Today, the various innovations and departures from received dance forms initiated by these choreographers are exemplified in the radical and experimental nature of contemporary dance. For instance, Martha Graham, acknowledged as one of the most influential founders of contemporary dance, developed a style that rejected the formal consistency of traditional ballet and modern dance as well as its setting and costumes. She evolved many techniques aimed at freeing the body and enabling it to express a wide range of emotions and moods. Merce Cunningham, who was trained by Martha Graham, departed from Graham's more ascetic style. He introduced what is described as chance choreography, emphasizing unpredictability and contrast in many of his works. He also created dances that were fundamentally abstract, against Graham's more narrative or literal compositions. Lester Horton, the African-American who founded the Dance Theatre of Los Angeles, and trained such great dancer/choreographers as Alvin Ailey, drew from Native American and modern Jazz dances to create his own distinctive dance vocabulary.

Although contemporary dance continues to be a heterogeneous and unstable genre, many of its choreographic styles are traceable to the works of these three pioneers. These styles, rather than any one technique *per se*, characterize contemporary dance not only in its US homeland but in its diffusion across the Americas, Europe, and other parts of the world. Defined by adaptability, receptivity, and structural openness, contemporary dance lends itself to appropriation and refiguration. As such, it has proliferated into many stylistic categories under the influence of local and traditional dance cultures. Its dialectical character of radically affiliating and remodelling at the same time accounts for its popularity among many contemporary cultures of the world. This distinctive quality, which has been described in hybrid and bilingual terms,[8] is an essential guide in our search for a contemporary Nigerian dance aesthetic.

Jane Desmond observes that cultural identities are embodied in movement styles. As well as pointing out that 'ways of holding the body, gesturing, moving in relation to time, and using space (taking a lot, using a little, moving with large sweeping motions, or small contained ones, and so forth) all differ radically across various social and cultural groups and through time', she argues that they can be transmitted either actively or passively from one cultural group to another.[9] These transmissions are typically transactional or dialogical. Instancing the transmission of classical Russian ballet to China, she observes that

> Chinese ballet is different from its counterparts in Europe and America not only at the level of movement vocabulary and syntax (i.e., what movements are done and the ways movement sequences are put together), but also in terms of choreographic method (where collective projects of choreography are not uncommon) and in terms of audience (ballet in China is conceived of as a popular entertainment). In addition, the narrative or story-telling aspect of ballet, which has dropped in prominence in European and American ballet forms since the mid-nineteenth century as more abstract styles have emerged, is a strong component of the Chinese repertory. Thus, far from representing merely the appropriation of a 'Western' form, the Chinese ballet produces a whole complex of meanings as well as formalistic innovations specific to its function in China.[10]

S.A. Ness identifies the same process in the Igorot dance from the Philippines which, rather than being an instance of 'cultural imperialism' is actually a 'decolonizing' strategy that employs a complex blend of movements from both ethnic and balletic techniques to forge a contemporary Philippine identity.[11]

Is it impossible, therefore, that this same process of indigenization of an imported dance style should replay itself in the re-situation of Euro-American contemporary dance into Africa? Is it possible that, rather than signal the triumph of Western cultural imperialism, contemporary Nigerian dance actually subverts its hegemony through a 'decolonizing' schema? After all Reed affirms that 'Dance may reflect *and* resist cultural values simultaneously.'[12]

## Contemporary African dance

In recent times dance scholars and practitioners have endeavoured to determine what constitutes contemporary African dance. This pursuit has been acknowledged as an uneasy one.[13] The classificatory difficulties that contemporary African dance pose constellate not only around the acknowledged nebulous nature of the phenomenon but also the wide range of identities that populate Africa. Our shared history of colonization and the many vicissitudes after independence further harass our every effort at self-representation. This figures most prominently because of the dreaded ghost of 'imperialism' which insinuates itself into our self-definition, engendering a kind of obsession which makes us often see its footprints in even the most unlikely places.

The search for a unique identity for contemporary African dance borders mainly on the issue of aesthetics – stylistic or structural consistency – and on ideological and thematic concerns. Having demonstrated how possible it is to practically and theoretically posit a typical genus of Filipino or Chinese ballet, unique dance forms created through a dialogic confluence of indigenous and European forms, the issue here is whether such a dialogic relation is possible in our appropriation of contemporary Euro-American contemporary dance. Are there discernible stylistic/structural and ideological/thematic idiosyncrasies exemplified in our appropriation of contemporary Euro-American dance, such that we can recognize distinct African threads in our own renditions?

Acknowledging first of all that Africa comprises diverse cultures, traditions, histories and peoples, the renowned Zimbabwean dancer/ choreographer, Gilbert Douglas, believes that there certainly is something of an abiding aesthetic across this diversity, and that a contemporary African dance aesthetic can be defined. He asserts, rather simplistically, that 'at the end of the day it [contemporary African dance] all relates to Africa. It is always African, and most importantly, contemporary'.[14] J. Pather warns that our reception of the imported dance style is diverse and therefore the question of an African aesthetic is anything but simple. Foregrounding the trauma of colonization, Pather construes our self-writing as a rather complicated and multilayered 'response' to that experience. He therefore wonders if our notion of contemporary dance is 'something that is derived from the fibre of our milieu or something that is actually picked up along with some faltering accents in New York or Brussels'.[15] His firm conclusion, nevertheless, is that 'African assimilation of Western techniques, materials, ideas and forms has been creative, selective, meaningful and highly original. The result is a continuous recreation of forms and style';[16] in other words, Pather believes in the existence of a contemporary African dance, a product of our diverse cultural identities creatively and critically engaging with our common backcloth of colonial legacy.

Interactions with some of Africa's contemporary dance makers who participated in the JOMBA contemporary dance conference in Durham, South Africa, in August 2004, reveal just how complicated this aesthetic is, and how widely individuated is the ongoing trialogue between received indigenous African traditions, Western orthodoxies, and contemporary individual sensibility.[17] However, what emerges in the various contributions of all the choreographers is that they are mostly aware of their fragile cultural positioning and are very much concerned with the danger of getting 'lost' in the dizzying whirl of cultural imperialism and globalization, and that many of them are consciously engaged in a process of self-representation or retrieval. Most of them acknowledge the necessity of engaging with their indigenous cultures in a desire to create a new dance aesthetic, to mark them out in the dynamic global range of contemporary cultural production. As African choreographers what they seem to have in common is 'an African aesthetic', conceivable stylistically but also ideologically. Adedayo Liadi hints at this aesthetic when he states that to him contemporary African dance is a 're-structuring of our indigenous African dance and bringing it into a contemporary framework through research, without being misled'.[18] Stylistically, I believe that this aesthetic is constituted in the manner in which movement vocabulary (and sometimes even syntax) is perceivably influenced by indigenous dance styles. Ideologically the aesthetic makes itself apparent in a decolonizing gesture – the need to continuously (re)define the self against the colonizing tendency of contemporary Western culture.

## Adedayo Liadi and the question of a contemporary Nigerian dance aesthetic

Although Liadi's response to his interrogator at The Place was directed generally at those Western connoisseurs of difference, he also highlights recent developments in the Nigerian dance scene where the typologies 'African' and 'Contemporary' emerge as contested, incommensurate, and often oppositional types. While 'African' characterizes a range of performance styles that rely heavily on traditional vocabulary, 'Contemporary' is more adventurously syncretist and reflexive and experimental. While 'African' practitioners are mostly characterized in official circles as the conservators of our culture, 'Contemporary' practitioners are generally considered saboteurs of our cultural heritage under the aegis of such Western agencies as the French Cultural Centre, Goethe Institut, and British Council. Some of the African dancers and choreographers are full- and part-time employees of the numerous State Arts Councils where they mostly perform decontextualized and minimally modified bits and pieces of our indigenous dances as touristic fare at official ceremonies and receptions for visiting dignitaries. There is also the National Troupe, a prestigious body comprising dancers mostly employed from the various geopolitical zones to reflect our diverse ethnic identities or 'federal character'. The Troupe is often seen as a form of cultural ambassador, performing at prestigious national and international occasions. This situation is not unlike the relationship between 'classical' and 'post-classical' dancers in post-1960s India as reported by Alessandra Lopez y Royo:

> Soon after independence, the classical styles became central to the modernist discourse and received financial support and patronage. Creative dancers – as the non-classical dancers were then called – did not enjoy the same level of acclaim as classical dancers. The underlying proposition was that, unlike the classical artists, creative dancers indulged in fusion work and this fusion carried a shade of negativity, for fusion and hybridity were seen both to be at odds with 'authenticity of tradition' which the classical dancers were perceived to embody.[19]

Thus, in Nigeria, while classical Nigerian dancers enjoy considerable official patronage, contemporary dancers have to source funding from corporate institutions and Western cultural outposts. At the same time, in response to their increasing popularity more professional contemporary dance companies are being founded. One reason for this growth in popularity is the conscious move by creative choreographers to increasingly evidence revisions of indigenous Nigerian dance techniques as well as contemporary realities which they share with their audiences. Many who are adept in the various indigenous dance styles began more consciously to creatively interrogate their response to both Nigerian and Western dance forms. Today, not only are there a number of contemporary dance companies being founded, but some originally 'African' companies have ventured into the contemporary terrain.

Adedayo Liadi founded Ijodee Dance Company in Lagos in 1998, and he soon became one of Nigeria's most successful and most decorated contemporary dance practitioners. With a powerful background in Nigerian dance, Liadi distinguished himself early on and won scholarships which enabled him to pursue formal training in contemporary and modern dance in Senegal, France, Austria and Germany. He has had many successful national and international tours, either as a solo artiste or with Ijodee Dance Company. For instance, 'Ori', his entry for the fifth African and Indian Ocean Contemporary Dance Contest in Madagascar, was first-prize winner in 2003. [See front cover] Other prizes/awards include Generalisimo of Culture (G.O.C), Lagos State Government, 1996; National Merit Award, Guild of Nigerian Dancers (GOND), 2001; Best Dancer of the Year 2001/2002, Guild of Nigerian Dancers, 2002; and two-time UNESCO/ASHBERG Bursary Award Winner, 2002-2003. Liadi has also worked in popular media, such as television commercials, music videos, and the popular television dance programme Celebrity Takes 2. He has recently been made the brand ambassador and the face of BESTLUB oil in West Africa, the first Nigerian dancer/choreographer to be so distinguished.

Originally Liadi set up Ijodee Dance Company to promote his career as a solo performer, dance teacher, and choreographer. In these categories he worked for many years with such professional theatre and dance companies as Centre Stage, Gongbeat, Ebony, Ivory Ambassadors, Tempo Productions, Black Marbles and the Lagos State Council for Arts and Culture. When he tried to enter for the fifth African and Indian Ocean Contemporary Dance Contest, he discovered that there was no category for solo entries so he had to set up the Ijodee Dance Center. Today Ijodee Dance Center hosts an international dance festival, TRUFESTA, which features local and international dancers, choreographers, and dance groups. These dancers and groups perform and conduct workshops in selected Nigerian cities and tertiary institutions.

While Adedayo Liadi has distinguished himself as a contemporary Nigerian dancer/choreographer, he acknowledges that finding his feet on the Nigerian dance scene after his various experiences of Western dance techniques was not a simple matter. In many ways his experience exemplifies the challenges in the search for self-identity confronting the contemporary African dancer/choreographer trained abroad in such Western dance forms as ballet, modern dance, and contemporary dance. He admits that at first there was a visible disconnection between himself and his potential Nigerian audiences: 'On my return to Nigeria ... I put up different shows of contemporary presentations. People said, "What is he doing? Is he stupid? Is he out of his mind?" Then I saw myself as an outcast in my own country.'[20] Even the dancers and choreographers he had worked with before he went to Europe for training marvelled at the manner in which he seemed to have uncritically adopted European contemporary dance culture. Liadi continues: 'Then I decided, "That's okay. Let me go deeper into my culture, into my roots. Let me go deeper and deeper." I continued researching for a new body language generally. Lucky for me, I was able to discover something new to show Nigerian audiences but still retaining my culture, still retaining who I am as a Nigerian, as an African.'[21] Today, Liadi is certainly a popular contemporary Nigerian dancer/choreographer, with a new vocabulary which his audiences find refreshingly captivating as well as recognizable.

A brief look at the award-winning 'Ori' shows Liadi's ideological and structural interrogation of his multiple exposures to different dance cultures and his contemporary life experiences. The first six minutes of the work clearly invokes the atmosphere of an indigenous Nigerian Yoruba ritual. It opens in total darkness, save for a lone naked flame fluttering weakly centre stage, and faintly outlining the curved back of a sitting figure. A harsh sound, punctuated by the striking of a metal gong, plays continuously in the background. It is monotonous, almost ethereal, and barely rhythmic. After a while, the lights come up faintly and reveal a man sitting with his back to the audience. Soon he swings around on his buttocks and a female voice begins to chant, 'Ori mi ooo!' The flame flutters before him while next to him at each side is a little white saucer. He wears a white loincloth made of the woven woollen fabric associated with the Yoruba god, Obatala, a white armband, and a white anklet. With extremely flexible, stretched, and measured movements, he picks up the lamp and executes a series of movements which give the impression that he is cleansing himself with fire. Soon he does the same thing with one of the saucers containing water, and then with the second containing sand. As he exits, a man bare to the waist and in ankle-length loose-fitting trousers is picked out in a spotlight. With a few staid and non-rhythmic movements he ends up kneeling centre stage. Two figures run past in front of him, one after the other. A young woman in a tank top and identical trousers is picked out in a spotlight upstage right. The man at centre stage struggles on the floor as if to free himself of some kind of bond. Soon another man runs in and stands in front of the woman. She exits as he executes a set of frantic movements with his right arm and foot, emitting a grunting sound and looking at the man at centre stage intermittently as if he expects an answer from him. Still kneeling, the latter looks up as if reacting to some kind of force above him, while the newcomer, now locking his palms together, begins to wind his arms as if he is cranking an engine. The woman enters again and stands in front of the man at centre stage. The man exits. She too reacts in alarm to the same force above her head. The invisible force becomes palpable and seems to toss her all around the stage.

These mechanically precise movements, with a series of entrances and exits, continue for a while until the five dancers end up together on stage. At this point two of the men and the woman are in a spotlight up left of stage, chanting and slapping the back of their hands into their palms rhythmically. Soon they are joined by the other two men from stage centre. Then leaning to their right they all look up sharply in alarm. This movement is repeated to the left, after which they begin to stagger about, twisting between and around themselves as if they are being tossed by the same force from above. A harsh metallic rhythm filters in progressively. The dancers scamper out of the spotlight and reassemble centre stage where another spotlight picks them out. Gradually they begin to run on the spot. The rhythm rises, sounding like the engine of a locomotive train. They run to it, looking as though they are running against a very strong current. Then, propelling themselves vigorously around the stage, they reassemble down right. From there they move into a series of energetic and tightly structured dance routines, that take them from one part of the stage to another. Some of the sequences consist of basic movements, such as swinging of the arms, strutting, and hopping, while others are technically sophisticated, involving dexterous twists and turns. They also carry out several routines on the floor. One of the floor routines is reminiscent of athletes warming up, with sit-ups and abdominal stretches. The music intensifies and the dancers emit vocal sounds in rhythm. At some point they all assemble at a spot upstage, murmuring in different Nigerian languages. The murmuring increases to what begins to sound like a heated argument. After a while the noise fades and a voice is heard speaking a recognizable Nigerian language. First it is gentle but soon it becomes more spirited. The dancers begin to crouch fearfully. The voice transits aggressively into a chant and expertly into an invocatory song. The dancers crouch into a ball on the floor as the voice fades.

'Ori' exemplifies both the ideology and technique of contemporary Nigerian dance. Firstly, although it is neither linear nor narrative, it clearly exhibits the unmistakeable influence of Yoruba tradition. The ritualistic opening with the accompanying costume, props, chant and music evokes an indigenous Yoruba religious atmosphere. This underscores Liadi's conviction that the indigenous culture should be researched and mined for themes and forms. Secondly, 'Ori' exhibits an eclectic technique, consisting of bland everyday movements, as well as intensely technical and tightly choreographed sequences. Although the dance routines observe some of the techniques of contemporary Euro-American dance, especially in the angular shapes and gestures, and unprecedented changes in both direction and dynamics, and the copious use of floor routines, there are very recognizable movements influenced by such indigenous Nigerian dances as *Swange* and *Bata*. The difference between the contemporary and the traditional techniques as deployed by Liadi is fundamentally implicated in the manner in which bodily movements are fitted to rhythmic and spatial patterns. While the indigenous technique is exemplified in strong rhythmic movements with limited floor patterns, the contemporary is less rhythmic and more spatial, deploying both aerial and floor patterns. Finally, there are obvious indexes of material everyday experiences. For instance, the babble of voices in local languages clearly brings to mind the socio-cultural makeup of the Nigerian nation and the ethnic politics that has beleaguered our search for national unity. Perhaps the subjugation of those combative languages by a powerful voiceover is evidence of Liadi's hope for a peaceful and united Nigeria.[22]

## Conclusion

Contemporary Nigerian dancers/choreographers are often charged by their critics with being wholly foreign or insufficiently Nigerian. In the main this kind of charge comes from a desire for authenticity; a desire to see indigenous Nigerian cultural dances in their pristine forms. However, the case is not that these young dancers/choreographers do not showcase indigenous Nigerian dance forms. Rather they creatively rework them with other dance techniques they encounter in their professional and everyday experiences. While for Nigerians who desire 'authenticity' this cultural eclecticism is liable to be objectionable, it appears that most contemporary Nigerian dance makers are quite mindful of the danger of being agents of cultural imperialism, propagating Euro-American cultures rather than their own indigenous and contemporary traditions. For Adedayo Liadi, confronting this danger is both an ideological and a technical project requiring not only a programmatic recourse to indigenous Nigerian cultural themes but a translation of indigenous dance forms into new vocabularies visibly influenced by Euro-American dances. In the first instance, the radically eclectic nature of contemporary dance positions it favourably for this kind of interrogatory project. Secondly, Liadi's mastery of both indigenous Nigerian and Euro-American dance forms is enabling to his professed aim: the 're-structuring of our indigenous African dance and bringing it into a contemporary framework through research, without being misled'.[23] Thus one finds in his themes and technique an invigorating trialogue between indigenous Nigerian cultural forms, Euro-American contemporary dance styles and the cultural, economic and socio-political challenges of living in a contemporary Nigerian cosmopolis.

## NOTES

1. Thea Nerissa Barnes, 'Ijodee Dance Company and Raiz Di Polon', *Ballet-Dance Magazine* (December 2004). <ballet-dance.com/200412/articles/Ijodee20041110. html> accessed 25 October 2012.

2. Olu Oguibe, 'Art, Identity, Boundaries: Postmodernism and Contemporary African Art', in *Perspectives on Africa: A Reader in Culture, History, and Representation*, 2nd edn, eds, R.C. Grinker, S.C. Lubkemann and C.B. Steiner (Chichester: Wiley-Blackwell, 2010), p. 352.

3. Olivier Barlet, *African Cinemas: Decolonizing the Gaze* (London: Zed Books, 2000), pp.

210-11.

4. See Ojo-Rasaki Bakare, 'The Contemporary Choreographer in Nigeria: A Realistic Culture Preserver or a Harmful Distortionist', in *Critical Perspectives on Dance in Nigeria*, eds, Ahmed Yerima, Ojo-Rasaki Bakare and Arnold Udoka (Ibadan: Kraft Books, 2006).

5. Erik Cohen, 'Authenticity and Commoditization in Tourism', *Annals of Tourism Research*, 15 (1988) 371-86 (p. 376).

6. See, for example, most of the essays in Chris Ugolo, ed., *Perspectives in Nigerian Dance Studies* (Ibadan: Kraft Books, 2007); also Yerima, et al, eds, *Critical Perspectives on Dance in Nigeria*.

7. Roderyk Lange, 'Anthropology and Dance Scholarship', *Dance Research: The Journal of the Society for Dance Research*, 1:1 (1993) 108-18 (p. 108).

8. Jane C. Desmond, 'Embodying Difference: Issues in Dance and Cultural Studies', *Cultural Critique*, 26 (Winter 1993-1994) 33-63 (p. 46).

9. Desmond, 'Embodying Difference', p. 38.

10. Desmond, 'Embodying Difference', pp. 51-2.

11. S.A. Ness, *Body, Movement and Culture: 'Kinesthetic' and Visual Symbolism in a Philippine Community'* (Philadelphia: U Penn. P, 1992), quoted in Susan A. Reed, 'The Politics and Poetics of Dance', *Annual Review of Anthropology*, 27 (1998) 503-32 (p. 514).

12. Reed, 'The Politics and Poetics of Dance', p. 521.

13. Loots Lliane and Miranda Young-Jahangeer, eds, *African Contemporary Dance? Questioning Issues of a Performance Aesthetic for a Developing and Independent Continent* (Durban: U of KwaZulu-Natal P, 2005).

14. Gilbert Douglas, Adrienne Sichel, Adedayo M. Liadi, Kettly Noël, Reggie Danster, Augusto Cuvilas & Faustin Linyekula, 'Under Fire: Defining a Contemporary African Dance Aesthetic – Can it be Done?', *Critical Arts*, 20:2 (2006) 102-05 (p. 104).

15. J. Pather, 'A Response: African Contemporary Dance? Questioning Issues of a Performance Aesthetic for a Developing Continent', *Critical Arts*, 20. 2 (2006) 9-15 (p. 12).

16. Pather, 'A Response: African Contemporary Dance?', p. 13.

17. Douglas, et al, 'Under Fire'.

18. Douglas, et al, 'Under Fire', p. 105.

19. Alessandra Lopez y Royo, 'Classicism, Post-Classicism and Ranjabati Sircar's Work: Re-Defining the Terms of Indian Contemporary Dance Discourses', *South Asia Research*, 23:2 (2003) 153-69 (p. 160).

20. Douglas, et al, 'Under Fire', p. 105.

21. Douglas, et al, 'Under Fire', p. 105.

22. See also my comments in Chukwuma Okoye, 'Postcolonial African Theatre: Notes towards a Definition', in *Developments in the Theory and Practice of Contemporary Nigerian Drama and Theatre*, eds, Duro Oni and Sola Adeyemi (Rochester: Alpha Crownes Publishers, 2011).

23. Douglas, et al, 'Under Fire', p. 105.

# The Language of Scholarship in Africa

## NGŨGĨ WA THIONG'O

Scholarship is not a neutral activity, even its conceptual vocabulary is ideologically weighted. Take for example the meeting between imperial European armies and resistance African armies. This is often described as soldiers pitted against warriors. Warriors are African; soldiers are European. Warriors live to fight. They smell, breathe, and dream of war. Soldiers fight in a time of war. They fight to defend territory, nation, or impose the will of their nation over another. Soldiers use guns, sophisticated weaponry; warriors, spears, simis and machetes, crude weaponry. Where soldiers shoot their enemies, oh, how civilized, warriors spear and hack, oh, how primitive. The imperial soldier is professional, rational in his calculations; the warrior is blood-thirsty, driven by impulses.

No matter in whose hands, scholarship impacts on how people look at and view social reality, including history and culture. For centuries, cartographers using a particular map projection have conditioned people to think that Africa is smaller than Europe. Yet, as some other maps have shown, Africa is bigger than a combination of Europe, USA, China, India, Argentina, and New Zealand put together. Scholarship started and helped perpetuate the notion of Africa north of the Sahara, including Egypt, as European, and Africa south of the Sahara as being Africa proper, with tribal hordes in perpetual warfare. Hegel emphatically declared that history, the enlightenment of reason and science, had bypassed his Africa which remained enveloped in the dark mantle of night, an image no doubt arising from his reading of colonial travel narratives that talked about 'Dark' or 'Darkest Africa'. Hegel's image becomes a truth in the grandiloquent ignorance of Trevor Roper of Oxford when in the 1960s he claimed that Africa had only darkness to exhibit prior to European colonial presence. Since darkness was not a subject of history, the history of Africa began with European colonialism. Some of these attitudes have changed in large part because of enlightened scholarship, but, still, the nomenclature of North and South of the Sahara, and the vocabulary of warring tribes, have become a given, more or less, in the discussion on the politics of the continent. Even when the adjective 'warring' is omitted, the word tribe has become enshrined in the annals of scholarship and popular parlance.

The other day I received a call – well, a suggestion – from one of my progressive colleagues at the University of California, Irvine, that we revive and rehabilitate the word and concept of tribe. He and some other scholars interested in Africa and Middle Eastern Studies had been chatting on how to reintegrate the subject of tribes into contemporary historical, sociological, and anthropological research and teaching on the Middle East, North Africa, and Africa. While the email acknowledged that the concept of tribes had a very problematic history for anyone studying the global south and the formerly colonized word, it stated that it was clear tribes as a social-economic and political concept and marker of identity were still relevant in many if not most societies we study.

The five letter word, again! There was absolutely no negative intent in the suggestion. Still, my eyes popped up. Two years ago I gave a lecture at the University of Hawaii on the myth of Tribe in African politics. I looked at how the five letter word had been used by scholars and journalists to editorialize how people looked at Africa. It was colonialism that first created the template of X-tribe versus Y-tribe as a way of explaining conquest and control or what Achebe's district commissioner in the novel, *Things Fall Apart*, famously described as 'the pacification of the tribes of the lower Niger'. Journalists use the template of X versus Y to explain any crisis in any part of Africa. They look at the communities from which the protagonists come, and everything becomes clear: 'It's the traditional enmity between X and Y. It is tribal warfare.' Even respectable scholars often use the same template, only theirs is covered with copious footnotes and references to Aristotle and Hobbes. I posed the question: why were four million Danes, or a quarter million Icelanders, a nation, and not ten million Yorubas, Ibos, or Zulus?

Even when scholars and journalists do not use the word nation in reference to European peoples, they at least refer to them by the names they call themselves. Thus they talk about the English, the Germans, the French, the Chinese, or, simply, Chinese people, English people. But, when it comes to Africa, the words tribe and tribesmen must be appended to the reference. Hence Yoruba tribe, Zulu tribe. Ibo tribesmen, Gikuyu tribesmen. An Englishman gets a Nobel prize in chemistry. He is rightfully referred to as Mr So-and-so, an English man or woman. An African gets a Nobel prize in chemistry, and he is editorialized as Mr So-and-so, an X or Y tribesman or tribeswoman. Novelist Ngũgĩ, a Gikuyu tribesman, was imprisoned by Jomo Kenyatta, his fellow tribesman. African heads of state must be editorialized as President so and so, an Y or X tribesman.

So my reaction to the email was quick and direct. Far from trying to rehabilitate the word and the concept, we should wage struggle against its usage. The same scholar, and I want to emphasize that his was an honest call, said that he had been to the Middle East and North Africa and found the term in use. In other words, people in Africa used the term. My first reaction was that even when people in Africa use it, it is simply because they have internalized a negativity. The abnormal has become normalized without losing its abnormality. But my colleague's citation of Qabila, the Arabic word for tribe, started me thinking.

The Arabic Qabila becomes Kabila in Kiswahili, and Kabira in Gikuyu. But even when those terms refer to the same grouping, as the English term, they have a different ring and nuance to them. They are more descriptive of a fact than a framing of difference in development and modernity. In my own language, the word *ruriri* has no connotation of negativity, being a reference to a community of people with a common language, land, and culture. The negativity associated with the terms tribe and tribesmen lies in the European languages, English in particular. The English word tribe in its colonial colours is a term of an outsider looking in at others.

I have suggested elsewhere that our various fields of knowledge of Africa are in many ways rooted in that entire colonial tradition of the outsider looking in, gathering and coding knowledge with the help of native informants, and then storing the final product in a European language for consumption by those who have access to that language. Anthropology, in its beginnings at least, was the study of the insider by the outsider for the consumption of fellow outsiders, and that attitude permeates the genealogy of European studies of Africa. We, the inheritors and continuants of that tradition, in many ways 'anthropologize' Africa, especially in method. Even within the continent, the Africa of colonial anthropology is seen as the true Africa. Pictures used by the tourist boards of various African countries are largely those of an Africa frozen in time. The complexity of the continent with its mixture of traces of past and present, the skyscraper and the shack, poverty and wealth, engineers and herdspeople, cities and wilderness, cars and cattle, is reduced to the spear and the lion, a beaded figure and the begging bowl. The bowl of the beggar overlooks the fact that the bowl of the giver overflows with goodies taken from the beggar's own granary.

This relationship between European and African languages is that of the two bowls, enrichment of one by impoverishment of the other. Today, we still collect intellectual items and put them in European language museums and archives. Africa's global visibility is only through the grace of European languages.

How many historians, African and non-African alike, have ever written even a single document in an African language? (At the Leeds conference, in response to my question as to whether any of the more than fifty scholars had ever written a page in an African language in their entire scholarship on Africa, only three hands were raised. For more than a page, not one hand was raised.) How many researchers have even retained the original field notes in words spoken by the primary informant? Our knowledge of Africa is largely filtered through European languages and their vocabulary. There are those of course who will argue that African languages are incapable of handling complexities of social thought, that they have no adequate vocabulary, in short, African languages, like their speakers, are riddled with poverty.

This point was long ago answered by one of the brightest intellects from Africa, Cheikh Anita Diop, when he argued that no language had a monopoly of cognitive vocabulary, that every language could develop its terms for science and technology. This is the position being maintained by contemporary thinkers such as Kwesi Kwaa Prah whose Center for Advanced Studies of African Society (CASAS), based in Cape Town, South Africa, is doing so much to advocate the use of African languages in all fields of learning, even in scientific thought. Other places with similar advocacy include that of the philosopher, Paulin Hountondji, at the African Center for Advanced Studies, based in Porto-Novo, Benin, which has tried to promote African languages as media for African scientific thought. There are other individuals such as the late Neville Alexander of Cape Town, South Africa, who chaired the committee that came up with the very enlightened South African policy on languages, and Kwesi Wiredu, who long ago called on African philosophers to engage issues in African languages. This advocacy has a long history going back to the Xhosa intellectuals of the late nineteenth century and continued among Zulu intellectuals of the 1940s.

All these intellectuals have tried to debunk the claims of the poverty of African languages, the inadequacy of their words and terms. It should not be forgotten that even English and French had to overcome similar claims of inadequacy as vehicles for philosophy and scientific thought as against the then dominant Latin. Those languages needed the courage of their intellectuals to break out of the dominance of Latin memory. In the introduction to his *Discourse on the Method of Rightly Conducting One's*

*Reason and of Seeking Truth in the Sciences*, Descartes defends his use of vernacular for philosophic thought against similar claims of the inadequacy of concepts in French.

I have tried to argue that what African languages need is a similar commitment from African intellectuals. It only needs courage and hard work exemplified by the case of Dr Gatua wa Mbugwa. Gatua wa Mbugwa was a graduate student at Cornell University and, in May 2003, he presented and successfully defended his Master's thesis on 'The impact of bio-intensive cropping on yields and nutrient contents of collard greens in Kenya' in the Department of Crop and Soil Sciences at Cornell. There was nothing unusual in this. What was new was the fact that the entire Master's thesis was in the Gikuyu language. For Gatua wa Mbugwa, it meant sheer dedication and lots of work for he had to provide an English translation. Later Dr Mbugwa joined the University of Wyoming where he did research in the US Central High Plains region recording his data in Gikuyu, and later successfully defended his PhD dissertation that he wrote in Gikuyu.

As far as I know, Mbugwa's work is the first ever scientific work in Gikuyu at any university in or outside Africa. He had no tradition on which to fall back, not even that of a stable scientific vocabulary, but this did not daunt his spirit. Most of his field work and field work notes in Kenya and the USA were in Gikuyu. He wrote the entire thesis in Gikuyu before doing auto-translation for his teachers who, of course, had to evaluate the scientific content. At present there are no Gikuyu language scientific journals or publishers. But he has published scholarly articles from his dissertation in English language scientific journals.

So what? Some cynics will respond and assert that Gikuyu cannot sustain a written intellectual production. I can only point out that the Gikuyu people are about ten million. The Danish are about four million. All books written and published in Gikuyu cannot fill up a shelf. Books written and published in Danish number thousands and fill up the shelves of many libraries. The Yoruba people number more than ten million. The Swedes are about eight million. But intellectual production in the two languages is very different. How come that ten million Africans cannot sustain such a production whereas eight million Swedes can? Icelanders number about two hundred and fifty thousand. They have one of the most flourishing intellectual productions in Europe. What a quarter of a million people can do, surely ten million people can also accomplish. Today we talk of Greek and Latin intellectual heritage and forget that these productions originated in city states. The vaunted Italian

Renaissance and its rich and varied heritage in the arts and architecture and learning were largely from the different regions of Rome, Florence, Mantua, Venice and Genoa. What the vernaculars of these city states, principalities, and regions by way of intellectual production have been able to do, can be done by other similarly situated languages.

The question remains: what would be the place of European languages in African scholarship? No matter how we may think of the historical process by which they came to occupy the place they now do in our lives, it is a fact that English and French have enabled international visibility of the African presence. But they have achieved this by uprooting African intellectuals from their linguistic and cultural base. They have merely invited African intellectuals to operate within European memory. European languages (principally English, French, and Portuguese) now carry immense deposits of some of the best in African thought and literature. They are granaries of African intellectual productions and, ironically, these productions as a whole are the nearest thing to a common Pan-African social property. The names of Samir Amin, Ali Mazrui, Wole Soyinka, Sembene Ousmane, Mariam Ba, Ama Ata Aidoo, Tsitsi Dangarembga, Sedar Senghor, Agostino Neto, Alex la Guma (to name just a few) are part of a common visibility of African presence enabled by European languages. These languages also enable conferences like the one we are having here today. The latter in fact defines best the mission we should assign to French and English. Use them to enable dialogue among African languages and visibility of African languages in the community of world languages instead of their being a tool of disabling by uprooting intellectuals and their production from their original language base. Use English and French to enable and not to disable.

This then is the challenge of scholarship in Africa today: How best to really connect with the African continent in the era of globalization? For African scholars, we cannot afford to be intellectual outsiders in our own land. We must reconnect with the buried alluvium of African memory and use it as a base for the further planting of African memory on the continent and in the world. This can only result in the empowerment of African languages and cultures, and make them pillars of a more self-confident Africa ready to engage the world, through give and take, but from its base in African memory.

In 1978, locked in a maximum security prison in Kenya for a work I had done in an African language, I wrote defiantly to my jailers asserting that African intellectuals must do for their languages and cultures what all other intellectuals in history have done for theirs. But non-African scholars cannot escape from the challenge. An English scholar, digging into the history and culture of Italy, studies Italian. The same holds for students of Chinese or Japanese history and culture. They study Japanese, Chinese. There is no scholar, Chinese or non-Chinese, who could ever claim to be a sinologist without a word of Chinese. But, in Africa and for Africa, on the whole, we claim to be scholars of this or that aspect of African history, culture, society, politics, without accepting the challenge and the responsibility. Scholarship on Africa has no alternative but to engage in African languages if it is to rise above the level of mimicry to contribute originality to the common stream of world knowledge.

In a note to the editor, Ngũgĩ remarked, 'It was a special pleasure to speak on the occasion because Leeds is my alma mater.'

# History, Intertextuality, and Gender in Ngũgĩ wa Thiong'o's *Petals of Blood*

## BRENDON NICHOLLS

In this article, I argue that *Petals of Blood* offers at least two models for anti-imperial history.[1] The first is a model of black world historical struggle. We might call this epochal struggle. The second is a model of Kenyan national struggle. We might call this a generational struggle. *Petals of Blood* is interesting, because in it we see Ngũgĩ's political vision widening out from a decolonizing nationalism to broader anti-imperial axes of identification. I think that this widening out can be traced to Ngũgĩ's University of Leeds research on George Lamming in particular, and to his wider reading in Caribbean literature more generally. It is useful here to recall that *Petals of Blood* is named after a line in Derek Walcott's poem, 'The Swamp',[2] and that it alludes to at least two of V.S. Naipaul's novels (*The Mystic Masseur* and *The Mimic Men*)[3] as the narrative unfolds. But it is the influence of Lamming in particular that we might identify with the making of *Petals of Blood*. In fact, Lamming's *In the Castle of My Skin*[4] might even be read as the genesis of a plot structure for *Petals of Blood*. As we know, *Petals of Blood* begins with the drought (mirroring Lamming's flood), continues with the journey to the city to protest to the MP (equating to the strike and the riots in *In the Castle of My Skin*), and concludes with a final phase in which the apparent marketability of Theng'eta results in the influx of corrupting economic forces and the establishment of New Ilmorog (just as Lamming's landlord Creighton has sold up and the new owners have decided to sell the villagers' homes out from under them). The death of Ngũgĩ's Nyakinyua before she loses her land mirrors closely the death of the old woman in Lamming's village before the Friendly Society and the Penny Bank evict her husband to the Alms House. Both novels mix third person and first person narration. Both interweave a series of perspectively-bound narratives that amplify each other's dimensions and build to the profundity of a fully elaborated historical perspective.

In Caribbean literature and in the black diaspora more generally, Ngũgĩ discovers a shared past of world historical proportions, and a community whose grievances and possibilities are global in scope. Within this radically amplified arena, *Petals of Blood* undertakes an aesthetic of reconnection in which Caribbean, African-American and African struggles for liberation are mutually informing and enlivening. Accordingly, the affiliations of *Petals of Blood* are diasporic, the scale of its ambition is epic, and I would argue that its structure has biblical parallels. This is no exaggeration. In *Homecoming*, Ngũgĩ writes that 'there is something about the Jewish experience – the biblical experience – which appeals to the West Indian novelist. Biblical man has been a slave and an exile from home'.[5] We should remember here that the Yeatsian section headings of *Petals of Blood* ('Walking ... Toward Bethlehem ... To Be Born ... Again ... La Luta Continua!') read like an extremely abbreviated account of Christian belief, encompassing the Jewish exodus from Egypt, the birth of Christ and, naturally enough, the Second Coming. What I think we have in *Petals of Blood* is a vision of socialist liberation as the realization of a faith in collective human potentials, and a vision of black world history as culminating in apotheosis. In this understanding, freedom crafts a god who may be recognized only in the dignity of other men and, we may add, women. Hence, *Petals of Blood* is, in one possible reading, nothing less than a bible of African world-historical experience. Its theology, if that is the right word, very precisely engaged with global Cold War politics, opposing itself quite consciously to anti-Communist Christian evangelism during the Cold War.[6] We might say that *Petals of Blood* opposes evangelical Christianity's ideological functions during the Cold War with a form of theological belief rooted in worldly institutions.

That leads us onto the second model of history in *Petals of Blood*. This second model is of Kenyan national history as a generational history of struggle. The novel is using an idea of generational history, derived from Gikuyu customary institutions, to think about democratic forms of political power. To understand this, we need to remember that *Petals of Blood* relies to some extent upon indigenous mechanisms of naming associated with circumcision and clitoridectomy. Gikuyu oral history was remembered via the significant names given annually to the circumcision age-sets, and these names link each generation to the significant historical events that accompany their rite of passage into manhood or womanhood. These processes provide one means via which Gikuyu oral history was remembered and retold. We see an example of this mnemonic history at work when Munira narrates his recollection of going to school at Siriana.

Siriana, you should have been there in our time, before and during the period of the big, costly European dance of death and even after: you might say that our petty lives and their fears and crises took place against a background of tremendous changes and troubles, as can be seen by the names given to the age-sets between Nyabani ['Japan'] and Hitira ['Hitler']: Mwomboko [a dance] ... Karanji ['college'?], Boti ['forty'], Ngunga ['army worms'], Muthuu [a dance performed before circumcision], Ng'aragu Ya Mianga, Bamiti ['permit'], Gicina Bangi, Cugini-Mburaki ['black market'].[7]

The names of the age-sets were given annually, after the harvest, so that Gikuyu oral history had a seasonal and cyclical pattern. As we can see, many of these names are Anglicized corruptions. Some allude to colonial conflict. For example, the Hitira age-set was named in solidarity with Hitler, a fellow enemy of the British colonial power. In its filtering of communal history through the age-sets, *Petals of Blood* is privileging a notion of generational history. When this history is viewed diachronically through its naming mechanisms, it gestures towards a lineage of struggle. The novel also draws on the Gikuyu custom of *itwika*, in which there was a peaceful transfer of power from one generation to the next, approximately every thirty years. This peaceful transfer of power ensured a 'democratic' system of government, because no generation could exercise power for all time.[8] There are signposts in *Petals of Blood* that it is reviving this idea of *itwika* as a form of cyclical and revolutionary democracy. *Itwika* was introduced when the *iregi* age-set revolted against a despotic king, following which power passed peacefully to the *ndemi* age-set who settled to cultivate the land. In *Petals of Blood*, Karega's name invokes the *iregi* age-set. Nyakinyua and her husband are of the *ndemi* age-set.[9] When, Nyakinyua refers to the corrupt Member of Parliament for Ilmorog as 'this Ndamathia which only takes but never gives back' (p. 116), she refers directly to the banishing of a river-monster (*Ndamathia*) by the Ndemi generation after the first *itwika*.[10] We can see here the narrative's blueprint for the revolutionary overthrow of the neo-colonial Kenyan government. Via its heroes of resistance – Ndemi, Kimathi, and Karega – *Petals of Blood* argues for the revolutionary institution of a 'democratic' form of Gikuyu government to replace colonial and neocolonial misrule. History here is generational, and therefore ultimately democratic.

Of course, generational histories require a vehicle of production. Implicit in this generational theory of political power is a rhetoric of reproduction which takes women's mothering capacities as its locus. But this rhetoric of reproduction is fraught because paternity does not work in this novel – the father's name will not stay still. To put this another way, the web of cultural and historical allusions in *Petals of Blood* makes the putative father's name multiple instead of unitary. In other words, *Petals of Blood*'s affiliation with wider modes of struggle (in the Caribbean, among African-Americans) means that we soon encounter a proliferation of signs that undercut the act of naming that ordinarily brings paternity and a male lineage into being.

I want to demonstrate this proliferation of signs in the examples of Abdulla and his Mau Mau comrade Ole Masai. In a discussion with Wanja and Karega about names, Abdulla reveals that his own name has its origins in a category mistake:

> Karega quoted the proverb. 'Somebody a long time ago asked the question: What's in a name? And he answered that a rose would still be a rose even by another name.'
> ...
> 'Names are actually funny. My real name is not Abdulla. It is Murira. But I baptised myself Abdulla. Now everybody calls me Abdulla.'
> 'You mean, you thought Abdulla was a Christian name?' Wanja asked.
> 'Yes. Yes.' (p. 61)

Abdulla's real name [Murira meaning 'one who asks'] poses questions and although his self-given name passes as a mistake, it quite fortuitously alludes to the dissident Kenyan Swahili poet, Abdilatif Abdalla, who was sentenced to three years imprisonment in 1969, for publishing a pamphlet entitled 'Kenya, Where Are We Heading?'[11] The name of Ole Masai, Abdulla's comrade in *Mau Mau* has similarly plural origins. Popularly known by the Gikuyu nickname 'Muhindi' (p. 137), he is the son of Njogu's daughter and Ramjeeh Ramlagoon Dharamshah, who occupied the shop prior to Abdulla's arrival. 'Ramlagoon' is, of course, an allusion to 'Ramlogan', the troublesome shop-owner in V. S. Naipaul's *The Mystic Masseur*. We are told in *Petals of Blood* that Ole Masai hates 'himself, his mother, his father, his divided self' (p. 137). His name denotes 'the son of a Maasai'[12] and his character is 'based in part on Joseph Murumbi (who is half-Maasai, half-Goan), a Kenya African Union activist educated in India [and the] first vice-president of Kenya'.[13] Where, then, should we locate the name of the father that Ole Masai hates? Is it Dharamshah, Murumbi, or Ramlogan? Is his name given by a Maasai, a Goan, or Ole's comrades among the *Mau Mau* insurgents? Equally, why should Ole Masai hate his 'divided self' when his comrade Abdulla's name is a mistaken Christian baptism and when Ole Masai himself descends partly from a picaresque novel by the Caribbean novelist, V.S. Naipaul?

We have trawled through a fair amount of fine detail and I would like to conclude with some larger propositions. The first of these is that *Petals of Blood*'s two models of history (generational and epochal) simply cannot work together. And the reason that they do not work together is that they occlude a key term – and that term is femininity in all of its agencies, varieties, and possibilities. For *Petals of Blood*'s ideas of generational struggle to work, we would need a stable notion of lineage. For a stable notion of lineage to work in a patriarchal society, we would need a stable idea of paternity in place. And the only way that paternity can ever be stable is via an act of unequivocal naming when the father claims the child for culture. This is something of a difficulty in a novel whose literary allusions and political affiliations are promiscuous. This is also something of difficulty in a novel whose key female character is Wanja, who becomes a highly successful prostitute in the final part of the novel. These difficulties are not insurmountable. *Petals of Blood* is profound enough and rich enough to answer them all. One possibility we might entertain when reading for history and for intertextuality in *Petals of Blood* is to turn towards a clandestine intertext in the novel – the covert history of female struggle in Kenya and especially the secret history of prostitutes who turned their revolutionary sexuality to the service of the Mau Mau struggle. By reading the novel against the grain in that way, we might exceed narrow rhetorics of reproduction and begin to comprehend new forms of revolutionary agency.

## NOTES

1. Parts of this article have previously appeared in modified form in Brendon Nicholls, *Ngũgĩ wa Thiong'o, Gender, and the Ethics of Postcolonial Reading* (Burlington, Vermont: Ashgate, 2010). They are reprinted here by kind permission of Ashgate.
2. Derek Walcott, 'The Swamp', in *Collected Poems, 1948-1984* (New York: Farrar, Straus and Giroux, 1987), pp. 59-60.
3. V.S. Naipaul, *The Mimic Men* ([1969]; London: Picador, 2002) and *The Mystic Masseur* ([1957]; Harmondsworth: Penguin, 1977).
4. George Lamming, *In the Castle of my Skin* ([1953]; New York: Longman, 1979).
5. Ngũgĩ wa Thiong'o, *Homecoming: Essays on African and Caribbean Literature, Culture and Politics* (London: Heinemann, 1975), p. 89.
6. See Billy Graham, *World Aflame* (New York: Doubleday, 1965) and Richard Wurmbrand, *Tortured for Christ: Christians Suffering in Communist Prisons* (New York: Spire Books, 1969).
7. Ngũgĩ wa Thiong'o, *Petals of Blood* ([1977]; London: Heinemann, 1986), p. 27. All further page references are to this edition and included in the text of the article. See Carol Sicherman, *Ngũgĩ wa Thiong'o: The Making of a Rebel* (London: Hans Zell, 1990), pp. 236-9, for a detailed explanation of the names of the age sets. All translations are taken from this source.
8. Jomo Kenyatta, *Facing Mount Kenya: The Tribal Life of the Gikuyu* ([1938]; London: Secker and Warburg, 1968), pp. 187-97. See also Sicherman, *Making of a Rebel*, pp. 166-7.

9.  Sicherman, *Making of a Rebel*, p. 166.
10. Kenyatta, *Facing Mount Kenya*, pp. 187-97.
11. Ngũgĩ wa Thiong'o, *Moving the Centre: The Struggle for Cultural Freedoms* (London: James Currey, 1993), p. 94.
12. Sicherman, *Making of a Rebel*, p. 228.
13. Sicherman, *Making of a Rebel*, p. 152.

# Interrogations of Law and State Legitimacy in the Theatre and Life of Ngũgĩ wa Thiong'o

## JANE PLASTOW

### Ngũgĩ wa Thiong'o and the Kenyan liberation struggle

This article focuses on two plays and a novel by Ngũgĩ wa Thiong'o. 1976 and 1977 were the two most productive years in the writer's life, in which he wrote the novel, *Petals of Blood*, and co-wrote two plays, *The Trial of Dedan Kimathi* and *Ngaahika Ndeenda* [I Will Marry When I Want].[1] The productivity came to an abrupt halt when the staging of *Ngaahika Ndeenda* by a community peasant company led to Ngũgĩ's detention without trial for a year in Kamiti Maximum Prison. I argue here that these three outputs and the events surrounding them, which put questions of law at their centre, were pivotal to Ngũgĩ's life and work, and key to transforming him from a realist writer heavily influenced by Western Marxist thought into a radical, African socialist, one deeply imbricated in the semiotic codes of his Gikuyu people, and operating as a Gramscian organic intellectual.

To put the work in context: Ngũgĩ wa Thiong'o was born in 1938 into a polygamous peasant family. Much of the wealth of his extended family had been lost as a result of British colonial policy which expropriated vast tracts of good agricultural land in the early twentieth century in what became known as the 'White Highlands', forcing Kenyans onto marginal lands or to work as landless labourers where they had previously been the owners.[2] From 1952, as Ngũgĩ's mother struggled to find the money to keep him in primary school, the Mau Mau guerrilla liberation struggle was the background to his life, with members of his family fighting on both sides.[3] Ngũgĩ became a fierce anti-colonial patriot, but one largely distanced from the struggle as, during the suppression of Mau Mau after the capture of Dedan Kimathi in 1956, he was away from home, having won a boarding scholarship to Kenya's elite Alliance High School, and by the time Kenya finally achieved independence in 1963, the then James Ngũgĩ was studying at Makerere University in Uganda.

Ngũgĩ began his creative career while at Makerere with his nationalist play, *The Black Hermit* (1962), and a number of short stories, but rose to international fame with the novels *Weep Not, Child* (1964), *The River Between* (1965), and, especially, the critical success of *A Grain of Wheat* (1967). The early realist writings are concerned with tribalism versus nationalism, and tensions between traditionalists and those who have taken on the religion or values of colonialism, but they are certainly not socialist. Marxism famously came to Ngũgĩ while he was studying at Leeds University from 1964 with a group of radical students and lecturers. Commentators, such as Simon Gikandi,[4] backed by evidence from Ngũgĩ's own account in *Barrel of a Pen*,[5] see *A Grain of Wheat* as hugely influenced by Frantz Fanon and the radical politics of *The Wretched of the Earth*.[6] However, *A Grain of Wheat*, which has as its central character a man who betrayed the Mau Mau liberation struggle, is deeply ambivalent about those who fought in the forests. Why then is *The Trial of Dedan Kimathi* and all subsequent writing so profoundly different in its portrayal of Mau Mau as a fundamentally heroic enterprise and its call for popular revolutionary overthrow of colonial law and the capitalist state?

**How to make an organic intellectual. (1) Listening to the people**
The Ngũgĩ wa Thiong'o who returned to Kenya in 1966 had been politicized by his contact with Marxist academics and by his disillusion with the neo-colonial government of Jomo Kenyatta, which allowed continued ownership of the best resources by multinationals and white farmers, and promoted the enrichment of a black bourgeoisie at the expense of ordinary Kenyans. He was also a realist writer sometimes seen, and applauded by the Western literary establishment, as much influenced by the Leavisite 'great tradition'. He was an academic intellectual who wrote beautiful, complex, measured literature, albeit from an increasingly left wing perspective. The production of *The Trial of Dedan Kimathi* was to change all that.

Firstly, the play is co-written, and with a woman, thus undercutting the idea of the 'sacred' text drawn from the inspiration of a unique elite individual. Secondly, it was a work that required the two playwrights to seek out the peasants among whom Mau Mau leader, Field Marshal Dedan Kimathi, had grown up in order to try to understand their man. This, it seems to me, was key. The playwrights discuss in their Preface how they visited Kimathi's village and met people who had known him.

> They talked of his warm personality and his love of people. He was clearly their beloved son, their respected leader and they talked of him as still being alive. [...] We went back to Nairobi. [...] We would try and recreate the same great man of courage, of commitment to the people, as had been so graphically described to us. (Preface)

What was radical in this was that Ngũgĩ and Micere Mugo were challenging the authorized written record which both under colonialism *and* post-independence inscribed Mau Mau as 'a savage and brutal form of extreme nationalism'.[7] Kenyatta's regime had no interest in valorizing popular struggle; rather it was busy propping up neo-colonial elitist entitlement. Of particular concern to Ngũgĩ and Mugo, therefore, was that the state was encouraging Kenyans to accept the colonialists' view of Mau Mau.

In *The Trial of Dedan Kimathi*, Ngũgĩ and Mugo are beginning to 'read' their culture through popular codes as opposed to elite literary knowledge. They are beginning to write through indigenous prisms of understanding that challenge authorized Western rationalist modes of literary production. In his autobiography and his accounts of discussions with ordinary people, Ngũgĩ makes repeated reference to popular talk of Kimathi's apparently miraculous powers.[8] The play seeks to incorporate and interpret such popular mythology. In the First Movement, Boy eagerly tells of Kimathi's superhuman feats, before Woman, who represents a true revolutionary, interprets the stories' symbolic truth.

> BOY: They say he used to talk with God.
> WOMAN: Yes. The fighting god in us … the oppressed ones.
> BOY: They say … they say that he could crawl on his belly for ten miles or more.
> WOMAN: He had to be strong – for us – because of us Kenyan people.
> BOY: They say … they say that he could change himself into a bird, an aeroplane, wind, anything?
> WOMAN: Faith in a cause can work miracles.
> […]
> BOY: Maybe they only captured his shadow, his outer form … don't you think? … and let his spirit abroad, in arms.
> WOMAN: Your words contain wisdom, son. Kimathi was never alone … will never be alone. No bullet can kill him as long as women continue to bear children. (pp. 20-21)

There is a mutual learning going on in this exchange, demonstrated in the dots and dashes representing pause for thought. The boy wants at first desperately to believe in the literal truth of what he has heard. His repeated 'They say … they say' both begs for corroboration from Woman and expresses his doubt about the truth of what he has heard, while Woman answers slowly and thoughtfully as she seeks to make clear her interpretation of the underlying 'truth' behind these stories. And gradually Boy learns, so that by the time he can differentiate between shadow and spirit he is beginning to see that Kimathi is both a man *and* an idea; and while the man may be caught, his spirit of revolution can live on in the

Kenyan people. It is as though the playwrights are also feeling their way forward, trying to understand a new kind of vernacular, one which tells its truth through an indigenous semiotic code. They are reclaiming both their birthright of popular Kenyan knowledge and a heroic Mau Mau heritage.

They are moreover beginning to reclaim language. After 1977 Ngũgĩ became famous for advocating publishing in indigenous languages as a means of validating and empowering the ordinary people of Africa as the primary audience an African writer should seek.[9] *The Trial of Dedan Kimathi* is the first time he experiments substantially with incorporating local languages into his text, making his work accessible to ordinary Kenyans.

## Colonial law and revolutionary law

The subject matter of *The Trial of Dedan Kimathi* is evident from the play's title. And indeed the moment that the playwrights keep returning us to is the reading of the charge at the centre of Kimathi's trial.

> JUDGE: Dedan Kimathi, you are charged that on the night of Sunday, October the 21st, 1956, at or near Ihururu in Nyeri District, you were found in possession of a firearm, namely a revolver, without a licence, contrary to section 89 of the penal code, which under Special Emergency Regulations constitutes a criminal offence. Guilty or not guilty?

Five times this charge is given throughout the play, but crucially no plea is ever entered. This is the 'real' charge made against Kimathi, somewhat absurdly the only 'proof' that could be pinned on a man whom everyone knows has been leading a guerrilla war in the Kenyan forests for the previous five years. What the playwrights do with this charge is to repeatedly challenge its validity by showing the thieving and torturing which epitomize British colonialism, until it is not Kimathi but colonial justice which is tried in the court of the theatre.

The first readings are followed by silence and a 'sudden darkness' (p. 3) out of which emerges the story, told through mime, dance, and song, of the oppression of Africans by white men from the earliest days of the slave trade through to the 1950s. We then go into the main narrative of how sympathizers are planning to smuggle a gun into gaol so Kimathi can free himself. A third reading takes Kimathi into a debate with a judge who first tries to argue that justice is neutral and universal before contradicting himself.

JUDGE: I am not talking about the laws of Nyandarua jungle.
KIMATHI: The jungle of colonialism? Of exploitation? For it is there that you'll find creatures of prey feeding on the blood and bodies of those who toil. (p. 26)

Unable to move their prisoner in open court, the regime resorts to a series of 'trials' which are reminiscent in language and form of the temptations of Christ; during which they seek first to bribe Kimathi with promises of power and wealth, and, when that fails, to break him through torture. None of it works, and the moral and legal standing of the court is utterly exploded. Following a final reading of the charge, and in line with the querying by Ngũgĩ and Mugo's original informants of any proof that Kimathi had died,[10] the playwrights utterly subvert colonial realist truth, by showing an uprising of the Kenyan people as they free their hero and take into their own hands the completion of a liberation process previously aborted by the execution of Kimathi and the sellout – as the playwrights see it – of the post-independence regime.

Colonial law is revealed as corrupt, and Ngũgĩ and Mugo contrast it with a demonstration of the law of Nyandarua forest. (It is of course deeply ironic that the judge should refer to the forest as a 'jungle', a popular site in the colonial imagination of African 'savagery', when we are about to witness both real justice and mercy in a location the colonialist cannot even correctly name.) Revolutionary justice is explored in some detail in the Third Movement of the play. In a flashback scene the fighters have captured two British soldiers and a Kenyan member of the King's African Rifles, and Kimathi arrives to try them. He starts with the British prisoners but the questions he asks are not about what they have done in Kenya; rather he wants to know if they are from wealthy or worker families, and when they say they are of the poor he goes on, 'Are you fighting for the working people of your country?' (p. 64) The soldiers do not answer and a stage direction says, 'They look at one another, confused, as if they don't know what he is talking about.'

The playwrights are making it clear that these men are oppressed, just as Kenyans are oppressed, by the imperialist class system. Kimathi gives them one chance when he asks, 'Will you denounce British imperialism?' (p. 64) The soldiers do not understand this socialist perspective, but when they reject their single opportunity for class solidarity they are led away to be executed. The Kenyan soldier gets no chance. He is immediately denounced as a mercenary. Neither poverty nor ignorance can be allowed as an excuse for betraying one's fellow oppressed. The playwrights are making it explicit in this scene that they are viewing the struggle not through nationalist but through international socialist eyes.

However the scene is not complete. Kimathi delivers a long speech about the need for vigilance and internal self-discipline to combat the propaganda and power of the enemy, before four Mau Mau fighters are brought in for judgement, accused of seeking to negotiate with the enemy. Most importantly one of the accused is Kimathi's own brother, Wambararia. It is in the historical record that this encounter really did happen, and, as in history, Kimathi extends mercy to these men who then betray him again and escape to the British. The message is clear. Family ties cannot be allowed to get in the way of revolutionary justice. To fight such a powerful enemy as capitalist imperialism, revolutionaries must understand the need for workers and peasants to stand together, but they also need enormous self-discipline and a justice system which cannot afford sentimental weakness in the face of the overwhelming odds it is seeking to combat.

If a debate on law is central to *The Trial of Dedan Kimathi*, it is important too in the novel which Ngũgĩ published next. *Petals of Blood* is also about dispossessed Kenyan people, but this time it is firmly set in the post-independence period. After a terrible drought the ignored people of the isolated village of Ilmorog march to Nairobi to seek the help of their Member of Parliament. He along with the pillars of the neo-colonial state whom the villagers encounter on their journey – religious, educational, and business leaders – all abuse the poor and powerless and refuse to lend assistance. The only member of the elite willing to help is a lawyer. This man is clear-eyed in his vision of the corruption of the state, and aware that even his legal practice which is run for the benefit of the poor is still part of an oppressive system.

> I am a lawyer [...] what does this mean? I also earn my living by ministering to the monster. I am an expert in those laws meant to protect the sanctity of the monster-god and his angels and the whole hierarchy of the priesthood. Only I have chosen to defend those who have broken the laws. (p. 196)

The unnamed lawyer gives the Ilmorogians shelter and valuable advice, and assists in the long term by lending books from his vast personal library to the young rebel, Karega. Later in the narrative, he becomes an MP. He tries as much as any man could to reform the situation from inside the establishment, using the establishment tools of law and learning. But for the new Ngũgĩ who rests his faith in the actions and knowledge of a united people, this intellectual, individual approach can only be palliative. The lawyer/MP is assassinated, and hope resides at the end of the novel in the beginnings of a trade union revolt inspired by looking back to revolutionary Mau Mau. Law for Ngũgĩ is not a neutral force but only as good as the ideology of the men and women who make it.

**How to make an organic intellectual. (2) Acting with the people**
Literary critical works on Ngũgĩ are numerous and mostly written in English. They focus almost exclusively on his novels. Relatively few Kenyan people had access to or were able to read his novels written in English so the Kenyan government had little problem with novelist Ngũgĩ even when he attacked the state. It was only when he started putting on plays that valorized popular heroes or critiqued the government, and most especially when he wrote them in local languages using local performance forms, that he was first detained without trial and subsequently forced into long term exile.

*The Trial of Dedan Kimathi* was staged by university students and was selected to be one of two Kenyan plays to be sent to represent the country at the prestigious FESTAC gathering of African theatre in Nigeria in 1977. Before the plays went abroad the playwrights wanted to put them on in Kenya and the obvious place seemed to be the National Theatre. In a lecture entitled 'Enactments of Power: The Politics of Performance Space', Ngũgĩ explains at some length how the white clique, which was backed by Kenyatta's government, and which still provided the theatre over a decade after Kenyan independence with almost exclusively European fare, only allowed the two Kenyan plays four days each to perform, and that only after enormous pressure.[11] He also discusses the huge impact of *The Trial of Dedan Kimathi*, recalling how, every night after the performance ended, the audience joined in with the final triumphant call for liberation and carried their celebrations outside in a mass outpouring and revival of revolutionary and Mau Mau inspired music and song.

They might not have been prepared for the level of impact of the play, but Ngũgĩ and Mugo use their drama not only to talk about but to embody the injustice of the colonial system. The stage directions are very particular about the layout of the courtroom. Stress is laid, for example, on the need to segregate the races witnessing the trial. 'Africans', we are told, 'squeeze around one side, seated on rough benches. Whites occupy more comfortable seats on the opposite side' (p. 3). The arrangement of the stage embodies the injustice of the stealing of space by white colonialists which gave rise to the Mau Mau struggle waged by the tellingly named Kenya Land and Freedom Army.

Ngũgĩ is himself acutely aware of the importance of embodying issues of space and power in his theatre. In 'Enactments of Power' he makes a number of references to Michel Foucault's *Discipline and Punish* (1979) and the state's desire to act out its power and the rituals of punishment.[12] Ngũgĩ and Mugo set up an enactment of state power in creating a courtroom and repeatedly reading out the charge against Kimathi but, in their case, this is done in order to make transparent to their audience state tactics for controlling the people and, every time the charge is read out, the courtroom space is subverted as we are transported to the stories which make clear the illegitimacy of the government and of the law in trying Dedan Kimathi.

*The Trial of Dedan Kimathi* is an African socialist play in that it eschews Western emphasis on the psychology of the exceptional individual and looks instead at representative types. Kimathi is only sporadically a particular individual; he is above all the embodiment of an idea, as are characters such as Boy, Girl, and Woman. White power is embodied in the figure of Shaw Henderson. Like Dedan Kimathi, Henderson was an actual person who, equal and opposite to Kimathi, represented all the evils of the colonial regime and its laws. He believed in the racial superiority of white people, was a dedicated hunter of Mau Mau fighters and, most importantly, was a torturer.[13] Henderson *is* British law in this play, taking on the roles of policeman, prosecutor, and judge. We see the British colonial and legal systems as monolithic and implacable but also as fundamentally illegitimate and brutal in their reliance on torture.

Building on *Petals of Blood* and, even more so, on *The Trial of Dedan Kimathi*, Ngũgĩ was to further transform his understanding of the role of law, performance, and the intellectual in the making of *Ngaahika Ndeenda*. This was a play Ngũgĩ wrote with Ngugi wa Mirii and the collective of the participants involved with the Kamiriithu Cultural Centre at Limuru. It was not a piece he had planned. Rather, members of Kamiriithu who were involved in an adult literacy course pestered an initially reluctant Ngũgĩ, simply because he was a local writer living near them, to help them write a play about their own lives, in their own language of Gikuyu, and using their song and dance forms.[14] Ngũgĩ produced a script which then underwent two months of modifications from the community actors before going into rehearsal. At the same time the community built a 2,000-seat open air theatre. Ngũgĩ says of this time:

> The six months between June and November 1977 were the most exciting in my life and the true beginning of my education. I learnt my language anew. I rediscovered the creative nature and power of collective work.[15]

The play he and his collaborators produced was set in contemporary Kenya, and told the story of how a rich Christian Kenyan family trick their poor neighbours out of all they have, a one-and-a half-acre plot, in order to facilitate the building of a foreign-owned factory, while their son is busy impregnating and then abandoning the poor couple's only daughter. Proper socialist thinking is provided by a group of factory workers, who come to the couple's aid before the community of the poor unite at the end of the play to vow unity in the mission to reorientate the nation and dedicate themselves to a revolution of the dispossessed. *Ngaahika Ndeenda* is a piece of impeccable – and often extended polemical – Marxist dialectic but in performance it is carried by extended sequences of song and dance and by the tenderness of the relationship between the protagonists, Kiguunda and Wangeci.[15]

Once more we see the law as a tool of the rich. At the beginning of the play, his title deed to the land he lives on is Kiguunda's most prized possession, hanging in pride of place on the living room wall. By the end of the play he has been tricked, as were Ngũgĩ's forebears, out of his land. Only this time it is not white colonialists but Kenyan capitalists who are impoverishing their compatriots. In three consecutive pieces Ngũgĩ has explored the workings of the law and concluded that law is no protection for the poor. It is not impartial but is manipulated by the powerful and needs to be recast to serve the needs of the working class.

This, the first Gikuyu play, was a triumphant popular success. A community was empowered and Ngũgĩ along with it. Nine weekend, fee-paying, public performances were packed out with bus-loads coming from all over Gikuyu areas of Kenya. Other community groups approached Kamiriithu wanting advice on how to set up their own centres, and new plays were being written by community members. Ngũgĩ is quite clear as to the factors which created what he calls 'an epistemological break with my past', and made the play resonate so powerfully among ordinary Kenyans. Language is first and foremost a factor. 'The question of audience settled the problem of language choice; and the language choice settled the question of audience.'[16] It was however not just the audience but also the community who made the play that determined its language. In *Decolonising the Mind*, Ngũgĩ explains how *Ngaahika Ndeenda* was created by the Kamiriithu community over many months as they witnessed, took part in, and critiqued the rehearsal process which perforce took place in clear view of the community whose lives it represented. The play became a mutual learning process, both culturally in terms of use of indigenous language and form, and politically in terms of developing understanding of the people's history and struggle against capitalist imperialism and neo-colonialism. It became, in fact, an exemplar of Frierean mutual learning through praxis, with the intellectual working with and serving his community rather than taking on the arrogant leadership role Ngũgĩ had critiqued right back in 1962 when he wrote his first play, *The Black Hermit* (1968).

In performance language is not, however, just a matter of words. *The Trial of Dedan Kimathi* had demonstrated to Ngũgĩ the power of popular music and song. In *Ngaahika Ndeenda* much of the weight of the play is carried by extended music, dance, and song sequences. He calls the play a piece of musical theatre, utilizing Kenyan performance forms, rather than relying on an imported European idea of theatre as privileging dialogue. Ngũgĩ explains:

> Even daily speech among peasants is interspersed with song. It can be a line or two, a verse, or a whole song. What's important is that song and dance are not just decorations; they are an integral part of that conversation, that drinking session, that ritual, that ceremony. In *Ngaahika Ndeenda* we too tried to incorporate song and dance, as part of the structure and movement of the actors [...] The song and the dance become a continuation of the conversation and of the action.[17]

Ngũgĩ is absolutely clear that it is the coming together of meaningful content, language, and performance form which made *Ngaahika Ndeenda* cogent and powerful. It provided a blueprint for developing a contemporary Kenyan cultural form which would reach far beyond national theatre buildings and educated elites. And it carried Ngũgĩ forward on his journey, foreshadowed in his condemnation of the self-indulgent, destructive, arrogant angst of Remi, the intellectual anti-hero of *The Black Hermit*, towards becoming that organic, native intellectual who 'has contributed to the victory of the dignity of the spirit ... [and] said no to an attempt to subjugate his fellows'.[18] And then the government stepped in, banned further performances, and detained Ngũgĩ.

## Law, justice, terrorism, and the critics

What the Kenyan government has done to Ngũgĩ and his collaborators after *Ngaahika Ndeenda* has been a succession of acts of state terrorism which in themselves go a long way to endorsing the political views he espouses in all the texts I have been considering. He was held in appalling conditions, without trial, for over a year after the banning of his play, and was only released after the death of President Kenyatta in 1978. In 1982, Ngũgĩ developed a new musical play, *Maitu Njugira* [Mother, Sing for Me], with a cast of 200 volunteers from Kamiriithu. This play never got as far as formal production. It was refused a performance license, and 'open rehearsals' at the University of Nairobi which resulted in wildly enthusiastic, overflowing audiences led to the banning of the play, exile for Ngũgĩ and his director, the forbidding of the villagers of Kamiriithu from ever putting on another production and the razing of their open air theatre. Only in 2004, when the government of Kenyatta's equally right wing successor, Daniel arap Moi, had been overthrown and a regime which promised more liberal governance came to power, was Ngũgĩ able to consider returning home. He went for a visit with his wife, Njeeri. And there, in an exclusive and well-guarded complex in Nairobi, unknown 'gangsters' broke in, raped his wife, and tortured Ngũgĩ, putting out cigarettes on his flesh. The perpetrators have never been brought to justice and Ngũgĩ has never again sought to return home. Kenya remains a committedly capitalist nation of startling wealth inequalities, and with little popular theatre or literature.

Ngũgĩ himself continued to write in exile. He now writes his novels first in Gikuyu before translating them into English. Theatre is obviously impractical without a Gikuyu community base to provide actors. He has also continued to write cultural and political commentary, and has led a centre committed to promoting translation from his university home in Irvine, California. He is greatly admired and widely written about and taught. But the admiring, writing, and teaching are generally limited to a consideration of Ngũgĩ's novels. The only book length study on Ngũgĩ which gives any substantial space to his theatre is Simon Gikandi's *Ngũgĩ wa Thiong'o*. Most other commentators either completely ignore or elide a consideration of the theatre, often with a few dismissive words about its inferior quality. It seems to me that this is not good enough. In his writing about culture and politics, Ngũgĩ returns time and again to the seminal influence of his theatrical work in influencing how and what he would subsequently write. It was theatre that brought Ngũgĩ to his understanding of language issues. It was theatre that transformed him from a realist to a symbolic writer embedding his work in the imagery and poetry of his peoples' culture. And it was theatre that finally demonstrated to him that radical change in Kenya can never be brought about by the efforts of even the most well-meaning intellectuals, unless they are truly working with their people. To ignore the events that drove and energized and created the writer and his works post-1976 is surely at the very least a mistake made by many contemporary literary critics. At worst, one might argue that criticism which does not take into account works the writer himself sees, and has repeatedly said, are seminal to his art is an attempt at cultural appropriation – with mostly Western scholars only choosing to approach the literature through a prism of Western understandings of art. If this were true it would surely be a piece of either unforgiveable postcolonial arrogance or an instance of postcolonial injustice.

It is the case that Ngũgĩ's theatre does not always fare well from a literary standpoint. It is full of long polemical speeches. Exchanges are often heavily symbolic and not naturalistically convincing, and there are all those stage directions asking for song, dance, and mime. What we need, I would suggest, are some new and brave critics of both theatre and literature; ideally, of course, Kenyan critics who can discuss the subtleties of the texts in relation to the cultural forms and language they use. But until they come along at least critics who might expand their reading outside the English stacks, or even leave the library altogether for a while, in order to understand cultural contexts, performance forms, and the political history. This will enable a critical voice to properly assist in the elucidation and analysis of Ngũgĩ's creative journey without amputating or ignoring the theatre which created that key 'epistemological break' with his earlier work.

## NOTES

1. Ngũgĩ wa Thiong'o and Micere Mugo, *The Trial of Dedan Kimathi* (London: Heinemann) 1976. Ngũgĩ wa Thiong'o, *Petals of Blood* (London: Heinemann, 1977). All further page references are to these editions and included in the text of the article. Ngũgĩ wa Thiong'o and Ngugi wa Mirii, *Ngaahika Ndeenda* perf. 1977. Published by Heinemann in Gikuyu 1980 and in English 1982.
2. In the early 20th century Lord Delamere acquired estates totaling some 150,000 acres. His descendant and the heir to the estates, which still come to 55,000 acres, Tom Cholmondeley, is currently on trial for shooting one Robert Njoya on the family estates. See <http://www.telegraph.co.uk/news/celebritynews/2224922/Lord-Delameres-heir-Tom-Cholmondeley-pens-account-of-shooting-poacher-in-Kenya.html#>.
3. For an account of Ngũgĩ's childhood, see his autobiography, *Dreams in a Time of War: A Childhood Memoir* (London: Vintage, 2011).
4. See Simon Gikandi, *Ngũgĩ wa Thiong'o* (Cambridge: Cambridge UP, 2000), pp. 98-127.
5. Ngũgĩ wa Thiong'o, *Barrel of a Pen* (London: New Beacon Books, 1983).
6. Frantz Fanon, *The Wretched of the Earth*, trans. Constance Farrington (New York: Grove Press, 1968).
7. S.M. Shamsul Alam, *Rethinking the Mau Mau in Colonial Kenya* (New York: Palgrave Macmillan, 2007), p. 123.
8. See Ngũgĩ, *Dreams in a Time of War*, p. 195.
9. See Ngũgĩ wa Thiong'o, *Decolonising the Mind: The Politics of Language in African Literature* (London: James Currey, 1986).
10. The official record says that Kimathi was executed in prison and buried in an unmarked grave. That grave has never been publicly identified. In the Preface to their

play Mugo and Ngũgĩ describe how Kimathi's friends rejected the idea that he was dead on the grounds that no-one had seen his grave.

11. Ngũgĩ wa Thiong'o, *Penpoints, Gunpoints and Dreams* (Oxford: Clarendon Press, 1998).
12. Ngũgĩ, *Penpoints, Gunpoints and Dreams*, pp. 54-57.
13. The real life Henderson is called Ian Henderson. He was a Scot who grew up in Kenya and became a notoriously brutal police officer. He wrote his recollections of the Mau Mau war with Philip Goodhart, *The Hunt for Kimathi* (Hamish Hamilton: London, 1958) before moving on to a thirty-year career in Bahrain where he became known as The Butcher of Bahrain. He holds honours from both the British and Bahraini state for his work in Kenya and Bahrain, despite demands from British and European MPs and Amnesty International that he should be held to account for his abuses of human rights. See <http://www.youtube.com/watch?v=ixMDcU40Tzw>
14. For an account of the establishment of Kamiriithu, see Ingrid Bjorkman, *Mother, Sing for Me: People's Theatre in Kenya* (London: Zed Books, 1989).
15. Ngũgĩ wa Thiong'o, *Detained: A Writer's Prison Diary* (London: Heinemann, 1981), p. 76.
16. Ngũgĩ, *Decolonising the Mind*, p. 44.
17. Ngũgĩ, *Decolonising the Mind*, p. 45.
18. Frantz Fanon, *Black Skin, White Masks*, trans. Charles Lam Markmann ([1967]: London: Pluto Press, 2008), p. 176. First published as *Peau Noire, Masques Blanc*, 1952.

MILDRED BARYA

# October

October home lying on the equator,
We had plenty of rain and sunshine
I don't remember
Whether days were shorter or longer
Nights always ended fast

Mornings broke
Dad holding keys to the storehouse
What shall we plant this October?
We were always selecting seeds
Planting. Harvesting. Grazing livestock.

I'm at the farmers market in New York State
I see pumpkins, pies, peas, potatoes,
Cabbages and cauliflowers
My father loved to weigh in his hands
How much does this cost?

I look into the White faces
But see my father. Always jolly
Proud of his crop.
Wiping at my eyes
I go to the one with the largest stall

That would be ours
I'd be the girl under the table
Picking from sacks
Arranging and replenishing
What I'm here to take.

# Going Home

The sea is the eagle that carries them home
Parting its wings and spreading the waters.
Salt treats their wounds
Where ropes and shackles have etched marks.
Water kisses the skin hunted and hated
As bodies fly down, down, in the grey vaults of history.

Waves the texture of soft fabric cover them
At last, they find cushion
A land opens beneath the sea and welcomes their spirits
They recognize home, Africa.
Whiteness no longer haunts
Dead and freed they are.

But the living continue to reel in terror
Every time a new ship arrives, guns and rum
Trinkets in exchange for kith and kin
First the invaders shoot the guardian angels
So folks wouldn't notice the vultures
Preying on Black faces.

# The Sink

Things easily rust with a little neglect.
Consider a sink, for instance.
Take a few days without rubbing and scrubbing,
you'll see how its lustre begins to fade.
A few weeks later, the colour you once knew is replaced
by a sickly, no, a deathly shade; the shine gone.
Blood, really. The sink becomes anaemic.
If you continue not to mind,
the sink will continue its way to rust and rot.
In between the rust and rot will be dust and dirt.
Once dust has formed itself into dirt,
and rust has coated the surface,
death hangs in the air like a comma,
leaving a little chance for intervention.
You can still rescue the sink. Cleaning restores its life.
Perpetual neglect brings the comma down.

SUSAN KIGULI

# Guilty
(Inspired by Mrs Dorothy Ongon)

I was guilty at four
Of loathing our mothers' sense of diet!
They knew nothing save for
Flaccid vegetables,
Sinewy pineapples and tangy oranges.

I was guilty at eight
Of thinking that all our mothers were
Fashion gurus, beauty queens, story storehouses
And boundless treasure haunts.

I was guilty at sixteen
Of regarding our mothers
Irrelevant, interfering women
With exasperating habits
Of mind reading, second guessing and disaster prediction.

I was guilty at twenty-four
Of suspecting all our mothers
Of incurable matchmaking
Of approving the world's most infamous nerds
For boyfriends
Of reminding us of family obligations.

I am guilty now
Of constantly praying for
Our mothers' safe-keeping
For hoarding all the cryptic comments
We received when ears heard
But hardly listened
For coveting the way they carry age like an accolade

For longing insatiably for their cooking
For their ability to prepare *Matooke, Malakwang* and millet
And to bake roast, cake and pie
For their defiance of hard times when
Sugar and salt were scarce
For their belief in their faith and values.
I am guilty of wishing to take all the soul
Of their generation to use it to redeem ours.

I am guilty of mother worship.


# Tulips
Rows and rows of
Red, orange and yellow tulips
In the corner shop
At Golder's Green bus stop
And a silly wish
To be allowed to sit
Among the flowers
Unobserved for a day
To touch their long petals
With my lips
To tease out stories
Of their life in the wind.

These tulips seduce
The eyes like sunset
Like goblets of red wine
Full rich red
Like glasses of white wine
Alluringly lascivious
I feel like a sommelier
At the mercy
Of their aromatic prowess.

# Amin is Dead
(For Peter Nazareth)

Like Buffaloes charging against the sun
Sweeping up dust to litter the sky
The news arrived
Via a friend then another and another.

Amin is dead.

What do you do with such news?
Then a joke came
From one friend and then another and another
A symbolic image of the man
Blood and laughter.

But what do you do with such news?
How do you weave into melody
Woes carried so long?
How do you put to rest
Grief that has never hoped
And will never.

How are we expected
To bear this news
To empty compounds
With graves half dug
To homes that closed
Three decades ago?
Where in the shades that replaced voices
Are we supposed to tell this news?

How do you expect us
To call our neighbours
Knowing that we no longer have any
And give them mats
So that we can exhume our
Grief and nurse it to sleep
So that we can wonder at the irony
That had a body
Children and wives
Who are sad now like we were long before
And will continue to ache forever.
A nation in exile.

Life is lost in mirrors these days
Three heads are standing on one neck
My mind floats
Between reality and disbelief.

# Divine Inspiration and Healing: Oral Poetry and Music in Uganda and South Africa

## SUSAN NALUGWA KIGULI

Many oral poets and musicians in African cultures see their work as divinely inspired and emphasize the cyclic nature of the relationship between performer, community, and the supernatural world. This article is based on interviews conducted between 2000 and 2002 with oral artists from the Zulu in South Africa and the Baganda from Uganda, and explores their relationship as poets and singers with the divine and with healing. For these artists a consciousness of the divine – whether Christian or resulting from indigenous belief systems – is very much part of their whole world picture, and they derive a sense of authenticity partly from these spiritual sources of inspiration, which link them to specific traditions, to a sense of place, and to their communities. Because I have been able to collect relevant interviews from a fairly wide range of oral poets and singers in Uganda and South Africa, and because these artists are eloquent in explaining themselves and their experiences as divinely inspired, I have chosen in this article to privilege the voices of the performers. I do not seek to judge their experiences, but to enable their voices to be heard as they told me how they experience their creative lives in relation to whichever divinities they recognize.

In Uganda, the performers I interviewed from Buganda frequently refer to their origin myths when explaining their understanding of inspiration and its link to the divine. Sam Kasule, in his discussion of ritual, indigenous folk forms, and the formation of Ugandan theatre, discusses performance and its connection to possession and trance. He explores the concept of possession and its relationship to impersonation and acting in the extended myth of Kintu and Nambi, the Buganda first ancestors. In the myth, Lubaale, one of Kintu and Nambi's sons, became a medium when Kiwanuka, the god of lightning, landed on his head, thus enabling his parents to commune with the Supreme Being, Ggulu, and the whole metaphysical world. According to Kasule,

In a strange voice, Lubaale talked to them about their past, present and future. Through him, they communed with Ggulu (Supreme God) and the other spirits in Ggulu (metaphysical world). After sitting for a long time, Lubaale went into a fit, collapsed, and then knew nothing about what had happened during the time when he was not in control of himself.[1]

The events of the myth are not only spectacular, but have a high sense of the dramatic, characteristics that are prominent in the narratives of divine revelation shared with me in interviews with poets and singers. Temporary transformation into another being is widely recognized as an aspect of being a Baganda medium.

> Among Baganda mediums, a person in this state may be transformed into animal 'caricatures', barking, snarling and howling. This transformation of medium into 'a non-being' underlines his multi-faceted character as the counsellor, judge, comforter, seer, psychologist, poet, musician, linguist and philosopher in his community.[2]

Spirit possession is seen as a state that enables a person to attain supernatural powers and acquire a new identity. This raises one's status above other members of the community and marks one as a vehicle for the gods' revelations. Poets I interviewed draw on this understanding to present themselves as people of knowledge not available to others, and therefore as indispensable to their communities.

Not all researchers are convinced by claims of divine inspiration. Isidore Okpewho, in his introduction to *The Oral Performance in Africa*, briefly mentions and seems to make light of some Nigerian performers' claim to links with spiritual forces.

> In my fieldwork among Aniocha story tellers in Bendel State, Nigeria, I encountered one who claimed that his box-harp [*opanda*] had spiritual origin ... Faced with these similar phenomena from three distinct cultural settings, the literary scholar is inclined to explore, not so much the environment of belief or religion in the respective societies, as the basis of such a claim before an audience ... *that the performer is simply trying to impress or affect as to the authoritativeness of his art.* [Emphasis mine][3]

Okpewho makes these claims sound like manipulative trickery, but I would disagree with this view. In my interviews I find the claims of divine inspiration made by the poets and singers are highly significant to their understanding of their role in society. They frequently link their inspiration to dreams and powers beyond themselves. One could choose to read this as the poets' way of representing their power of imagination, but they undoubtedly see themselves as vehicles of divine revelation rather than as mere individuals creating art. They also see this spiritual link as granting them the right to act as spokespersons in their communities, and their performance as an embodiment of the interrelationship between individual, community, and the divine.

Some narratives presented by poets can sound extraordinary when read outside their home context, but it is surely significant that the poets believe in their perspective sufficiently strongly to present it for academic analysis. To my mind, the recurrence of related views expressed by poets from across a wide geographical area, and from different ethnic and cultural backgrounds, mean that they must be taken seriously. These interviews become important in interpreting how songs and poems 'mean', and are manifested in performance as part of the power of belief systems and traditions.

Performers in Kwazulu Natal link their inspiration directly to the ancestors and the divine realm. When I ask the *imbongi* [praise poet], Peuri Dube, about the source of his inspiration and interest in poetry, he says,

> One day when I was asleep at night, men appeared to me in a dream and commanded me to start praising but I did not ask them who I was to praise; they just commanded me and gave me a short stanza to perform. I praised and they approved and disappeared. Then on another night they came again and commanded me to praise the man again. I talked to my mother and told her about the dreams and the fact that men had told me to praise the same man every morning again and again ... the man's name is King Cetswayo.[4]

This is a typical example of how the poets experience their lives as deeply connected to the spiritual, social, and historical structures of their communities. Their poetic lives are inseparable from the 'real life' of the community in which they live and perform. Dube is not *imbongi* to the current Zulu king, Goodwill Zwelithini, but he has performed before him on several occasions. He recalls one of these in the following manner.

> I dream about things and they happen. Before King Zwelithini visited Durban in 1998, men came to me in a dream and told me I was going to perform for the king ...There was a function and I welcomed him, because it is our custom that before the king speaks an *imbongi* must lead him. I performed King Shaka's praise poem. It was Heritage Day therefore I performed the praises of the founder of the nation, King Shaka. *I have learnt a lot of things about our culture. You see these days everyone wants to come with their own style. They claim they learnt these things in school. They tell you that they went to London, to Germany to learn these things then you cannot oppose them.* [Emphasis mine][5]

In fact, of course, Dube is here trumping any Western knowledge with his claims of divine inspiration. But he is also asserting the importance of his culture, place, and history as opposed to globalized knowledge. Given the history of apartheid and Zulu cultural nationalism it is not surprising that local cultural forms have assumed considerable importance and prestige. They are not only spiritually important, but a means of resisting

Westernization, and promoting self-confidence and pride in Zulu identity.

However, not all poets will claim that their inspiration comes from the ancestors or from indigenous divinities. One group attribute their inspiration to the Christian God. Phila Myeni is a member of the Durban Christian Centre, a Pentecostal church. His discussion of divine inspiration is strikingly similar to that of Dube and other oral poets, but in his case he refers to the action of the Holy Spirit.

> So this poetry came to me almost like in a dream and inspired me. I rely on inspiration, on the Spirit, I believe in God, I believe in the teachings of the Holy Spirit, because I did not go to school for poetry or to art school to learn these things. I just rely on the inner me to do these things.[6]

Like Dube and Myeni, a number of the South African poets I interviewed dwell on not having completed formal education. Instead they speak of learning from other oral poets and of divine revelation; these are the alternative sources which authorize their activity and give them power in their communities.

God may also be seen as bestowing creative poetic talent. Damascus Ssali, a poet from Buganda, explains as follows:

> The strategies used by any poet are influenced by talent. God gives talent to people and composition involves talent. You compose the action as well as the voice rendition. Some people have talent in using their voices as well as the gestures. In Luganda poetry (which I live with), the voice and gestures shape the content. As I said before, pulse in our poetry is important. To master these methods, I believe you have to possess the power communicated by the voices of the ancestors, it is divine power.[7]

His view is supported by, first, poet Thembisile Myathaza, and then *maskanda*[8] musician, Siphiwe Cele, from South Africa.

> My poetry comes in phases. There is something that descends on me and tells me to compose about a particular subject ... It is the talent. I realize that I have got the talent. Whenever I am going to perform, I first thank God for this gift because I take it as a gift. It is something I cannot run away from. It is in me. It makes me see and sift images, if you like, it drives me to evaluate as well as make connections between events.[9]

> As far as I know *maskanda* is a natural gift that my ancestors have given to me. You know you are born with your hands folded in a fist and so these gifts come folded in your fist at birth. It is a natural gift, a talent coming from inside me. But I cannot deny that observing and learning from others has improved my style. It has sharpened my skills and made me think more about how I play.[10]

The latter comment develops some of the thinking expressed by other poets and singers. All my interviewees argue that their poetic musical talent is divinely inspired and all are strongly aware of the power of the sacred. But Cele is also acknowledging that the divine gift can be developed by instruction and critical thought. This dual awareness helps explain why many poets treat inspiration and composition as two related but distinct processes.

Moses Serwadda, a performer from Buganda and music lecturer, tells me that dreams are a common way for poets and singers to receive their inspiration. He recites a long narrative folk poem, *Geya Geyanga*, in which the persona dreams about the dangers of laziness. In the poem, which is translated below, dreams are used to teach the dreamer to avoid being lazy.

Excerpt from *Geya Geyanga*
*Geya geyanga*
*Bwenali nga nebisse*
*Geya geyanga*
*Otulo netukwata*
*Geya geyanga*
*Ng'o tulo tunsimbye*
*Geya geyanga*
*Nefuluta nekamala*
*Geya geyanga*
*Ebirooto n'ebyesomba*

After covering myself with the bedclothes
*Geya geyanga*
I fell asleep
*Geya geyanga*
After sleep had paralysed me
*Geya geyanga*
I snored uncontrollably
*Geya geyanga*
After sleep had trapped me
*Geya geyanga*
Dreams came in great numbers

According to Sserwadda, dreams are one way of seeing in images and therefore have a very close connection with poetry. Furthermore most of the performers I interviewed speak of dreams as giving them not only a mandate but an imperative command to practise poetry and/or song creation. The female Muganda oral poet, Phoebe Nakibuule Mukasa, explains how she sees the link between dreams, divine inspiration, and the creation of oral poetry, once more praising indigenous sources of knowledge above international scholarship.

Oral poets in my view are more powerful than the ones who write. The oral poet's selection of words is stronger than that of the poets who write. The oral poets feel that a poem should sound a certain way. Our people in Buganda have a fear of writing but when composing orally they feel freer. *Do you know that people still see visions? There are people who see visions. Someone may keep silent and hear voices. There was a famous poet in the 1950s called Bugembe. He had that gift, in fact he just disappeared, no one knows his whereabouts.* He sang the famous song *Bulange.* This man was a great musician and poet. In fact Ssekabaka Muteesa II wanted him to go to Britain to study music and he offered him a scholarship. Bugembe went to the King and begged him not to send him away from home ... He told the King that sending him to England would not make him a better poet or singer. He revealed that whenever he wanted to produce a poem or song, he had just to climb up the top of Mutundwe hill and he would be able to come up with a composition. [Emphasis mine][11]

Some poets believe that there is a specific spiritual link between themselves and a spirit or alter ego living in the spirit world. The South Africans, Dube and Pitika Ntuli, both have a strong sense of this other being who works with and through them.

I believe it is not me when I praise; it is someone behind me who is doing this. It is not me who composed this poem; it is a spirit which tells me what to do. My name is Peuri but it is not me. Peuri represents someone in the other world but you cannot see that person.[12]

I am here as Pitika but there is another Pitika in the spiritual world who exists with other people who advise him...The patrilineal and matrilineal lines, of the *amatongo* [ancestors] are actually looking after me and they guide me.[13]

The experience of these poets and singers clearly cannot be rationally explained, but the body of evidence I collected in both Uganda and South Africa relating to the creative lives of these artists, seems to me important. However Western science or psychoanalysis may seek to explain these experiences – and, as we have seen, a Western-trained African analyst such as Okpewho may write off such stories as self-aggrandizing trickery – my evidence is that divine inspiration, often through dreams, is powerfully experienced by many leading African oral poets and singers. One of my most precise and extraordinary stories, resulting in the creation of a new musical instrument, came from Muganda musician, Ssennoga Majwara.

The story I am about to tell you is a bit difficult to tell and believe. I had gone to Mityana to supervise some of my students who were on school practice. I was alone in my room, awake reading, and then around one or two o'clock (maybe I had dropped off to sleep) I saw myself playing an instrument and I could not recognise it from before. I wondered about it and eventually realised it was a type of xylophone. I was playing it and the song I was playing sounded complete. I woke up and realised that it was a dream. I then went back to sleep and just about ten minutes later I had exactly the same dream. I saw this instrument again and I was playing it alone. I produced a whole song. I looked intently at this instrument and saw it very clearly. It looked real. I woke up again as if from another world. I got a piece of paper and drew a sketch of it just as I had seen it in the dream. I went to our xylophone maker Mr Ssebuwufu and I explained in detail what I wanted him to make and he made it.[14]

## South African praise poetry as a channel for healing

My view is that the praise poem has power to heal the nation. The TRC had the mandate to expose evil but the praise poem has the power to heal.[15]

The latter part of this article discusses a specifically South African phenomenon; the strong link made by praise poets from Kwazulu Natal between poetry and healing and the nation. Given that my research was conducted not long after the powerful, if at times controversial, work of the South African Truth and Reconciliation Commission (TRC) between 1996 and 1998, it is not surprising that national healing was a major concern at the time for many.

Apartheid inflicted wounds of inconceivable magnitude, particularly on the black South African populace, and, since 1996, the post-apartheid rhetoric of reconciliation has come to be symbolized by the TRC. The Commission was set up with the aim of promoting the reconstruction and reconciliation of the fractured South African polity using historical facts, records, and individual and collective testimonies. It aimed to recapture the stories of victims and perpetrators in order to enable the country to confront and come to terms with its history and legacy. As Archbishop Desmond Tutu, the Chairman of the TRC, notes in his foreword to the final report, the Commission saw itself as part of a process of national healing.

The commission has not been prepared to allow the present generation of South Africans to grow gently into the harsh realities of the past and, indeed, many of us have wept as we were confronted with its ugly truths. However painful the experience has been, we remain convinced that *there can be no healing without truth* ... However painful, the experience, the wounds of the past must not be allowed to fester. They must be opened. They must be cleansed. *And balm must be poured on them so they can heal.* This is not to be obsessed with the past. It is to take care that the past is properly dealt with for the sake of the future. [Emphasis mine][16]

The TRC was widely viewed as part of healing post-apartheid South Africa. All the Zulu poets I interviewed in depth, as the evidence shows, refer to it as an important institution which helps people look again at South African history, as well as assisting them in evaluating clashes between the Inkatha Freedom Party (IFP), the United Democratic Front (UDF) and, later, the African National Congress (ANC) that happened in

Kwazulu Natal and on the East Rand. However a number of the poets also insist that the TRC could expose evil but could not effect healing.

To poets such as Peuri Dube healing is a process that involves more than testimony. It requires the naming of the brave ancestral spirits, placing events in a wide historical context, and invoking the active participation of the audience. He asserts that praise poetry not only evokes the power of the ancestors, but also creates an intimate link between the mind and the voice through the creation of powerful imagery and rhythm. He goes on to argue that the atmosphere of a performance poetry event is radically different from the dry reports and interrogation of the TRC. It could give a voice to the trauma suffered under apartheid, could drain a person's anger, and open up possibilities of release from pain. Unlike the formal, official face of the TRC, an oral poetry performance could benefit from being in a form familiar to audience members, creating an atmosphere of confidence and strength for both performer and audience.

The female praise poet, Thembisile Myathaza, explains how for her the composing of poetry has been a healing experience.

> Poetry in my opinion is about remembering, inscribing experiences onto the stage for wider evaluation. I have composed a poem that remembers the time when I was staying in Lingeland when there were many riots going on and because we were Xhosas, my mother had moved there because of urbanisation ... I would visit my mother during the holidays. But when we would be going to the bus stop, people in the riots would call us names, for example 'seed of Mandela', they belonged to IFP. It was a frightening experience that left me shaken, but now because I am composing poetry I have thought about this experience and I think it was really foolish. Poetry has rid me of my fear, it was as if composing and performing a poem about the experience washed me and released me from fear.[17]

Poetry has been crucial in helping Myathaza understand her situation, and Phila Myeni has a similar experience.

> Praise poetry in my view facilitates healing of say, trauma, so I created this platform in the hope that we could use it as a vehicle of expression for as many people as we could reach in this community. What I experienced when I started composing poetry is that it healed me. When I was on crutches from gunshot wounds, the poetry I composed kept me going ... In my poetry, both the praise poems and my social poetry; I want to feel that it is healing poetry ... I have overcome confusion and bitterness so I take my poetry as a way of trying to heal people emotionally.[18]

Myeni argues that, as poetry composition has benefitted him, so it can help others, both through encouraging them to create their own works and through sharing the emotional journey of a poem. This poetry explores the brutality experienced by, and the exploitation of, the black population under apartheid. It made 'tangible' past wrongs, and allowed painful issues to be opened up for public discussion. Because praise poetry utilizes historical and cultural contexts held in common by many Zulu people, it is regarded as particularly valuable in enabling people to see their sufferings within a 'national' narrative. Pitika Ntuli powerfully summarizes his understanding of the power of praise poetry for his people.

> I think a praise poet is the guardian of historical memory, a witness to the times in which we live, a conscience of the community as well as a soldier at the frontline to bring change in the nation, and the best weapon is the words, voice and collective memory.[19]

## NOTES

This article is adapted from the research which resulted in my PhD, *Oral Poetry and Popular Song in Post-Apartheid South Africa and Post-Civil War Uganda: A Comparative Study of Contemporary Performance,* unpublished PhD thesis, University of Leeds, 2004.

1. Samuel Kasule, *Traditional and Contemporary Influences upon Uganda Theatre between 1960 and 1990,* unpublished PhD thesis, University of Leeds, 1993, p. 4.
2. Kasule, *Traditional and Contemporary Influences,* p. 6.
3. Isidore Okpewho, ed., *The Oral Performance in Africa* (Ibadan: Spectrum, 1990), p. 7.
4. Interview with Peuri Dube, Kwamuhle Museum, Durban, 30 November 2001.
5. Interview, Dube, 30 November 2001.
6. Interview with Phila Myeni, Kwamashu, Kwazulu Natal, 10 December 2001.
7. Interview with Damascus Ssali, Bulange Mengo, 27 July 2001.
8. *Maskanda* music is an immensely popular style in Kwazulu Natal. It is a form that not only uses *izibongo* [praise poetry] in its songs but is seen as being intimately connected with Zulu identity. *Maskanda* focuses on the mixing of styles while maintaining close links with Zulu traditional forms of poetical and musical expression.
9. Interview with Thembesile Myathaza, Vuma Arts Centre, Durban, 20 November 2001.
10. Interview with Siphiwe Cele, Vuma Arts Centre, Durban, 12 October 2001.
11. Interview with Phoebe Nakibuule Mukasa, Bulange, 03 August 2001.
12. Interview, Dube, 30 November 2001.
13. Interview, Pitika Ntuli, African Renaissance Development Institute, Durban, 17 November 2001.
14. Interview with Ssenoga Majwara, Kyambogo, 10 September 2001.
15. Interview, Dube, 30 November 2001.
16. The TRC Report Extract 1 Supplement, Independent Newspapers and Idasa, 2 November 1998, p. 2.
17. Interview, Myathaza, 20 November 2001.
18. Interview, Myeni, 10 December 2001.
19. Interview, Ntuli, 17 November 2001.

# 'Bye-bye *Nyakatsi*': Life through Song in Post-Genocide Rwanda

## ANDREA GRANT

I don't remember the first time I heard the song 'Bye-bye *Nyakatsi*' ['Bye-bye Thatch-roofed Houses'] by the Rwandan rapper, Bulldogg. Like so much of my fieldwork into popular music in Rwanda, there was no '*aha*' moment of revelation, but rather a long, slow, almost unconscious accumulation of familiarity. Crammed into the backseat of a public bus, I'd find myself singing along to a Kinyarwanda chorus blaring from tinny speakers, inevitably only a few inches from my ears, with no recollection of how or where I'd learnt it. (Much to the stifled chuckles, I should note, of my fellow passengers.) In Kigali, Kinyarwanda-language music – be it hip hop, rap, R&B, gospel, or Afropop – was the ever-present soundtrack to young peoples' lives, the rhythms to which they carried out their various *gahunda* [programmes] in the city. Spend enough time with them – hanging out at their homes sipping warm Fantas; sharing goat brochettes at hidden cabarets down the dusty back-roads of Nyamirambo, Kigali's so-called 'ghetto'; attending one of the various 'play-back' concerts that took place at crowded hotel bars every weekend; or, indeed, taking any form of public transportation, anywhere – you were bound to pick up something. You listened with more than your ears; with your body, through the skin, a sort of musical osmosis.

With the opening up of the country's airwaves in 2004 and the ensuing proliferation of private radio stations, the music and entertainment industry in Rwanda has boomed. Some of the country's most popular radio programmes are centred on entertainment [*imyidagaduro*] and dozens of paparazzi-style celebrity websites have popped up, documenting the private lives of the country's most famous young 'stars' [*abastar* or, less colloquially, *abahanzi*, performers or musicians]. This is not to imply that friends didn't nod their heads along to the latest track by Rihana or P-Square, or relish the misadventures of American celebrities, such as Lady Gaga or Kim Kardashian – they did. But they also reserved a special place in their *imitima* [hearts] for Kinyarwanda-language popular music, especially rap and hip hop. To them, this new music spoke 'the truth' [*ukuri*]. Songs like 'Bye-bye *Nyakatsi*' articulated the hardships, uncertainties, and hedged aspirations of young people in Kigali, especially young men, where the gains of development and progress never seemed to trickle down to them. Bulldogg wasn't a member of the hip hop crew called Tuff Gang for nothing. As one young fan told me, explaining why he admired the music of Jay Polly, another popular Rwandan rapper and member of Tuff Gang, 'The message – he gives the message to work hard and live peacefully, especially for small people.'

Although I could have picked another song from the dozens available – the stereotype of Rwanda as 'the quietest country … in sub-Saharan Africa'[1] dissolves the moment one leaves behind the gated communities of the elite neighbourhoods of Nyarutarama and Gaculiro – I'm choosing to focus on 'Bye-bye *Nyakatsi*' and the multiple semantic resonances it created. Bulldogg has other, arguably more well-known songs – 'Customer Care', for example, a humorous take on the country's campaign to improve customer service – and there are other rappers considered more famous. But 'Bye-bye *Nyakatsi*' is significant – and surprising – because it evokes and seems to challenge, however cryptically, the country's unequal socio-political system and corrupt moral economy. More importantly, it carves out a space for young people to reflect upon this 'deception' and critically engage with the discourses, processes, and effects of state-controlled 'development' and 'modernization'. For Bye-bye Nyakatsi was also the name of a controversial government policy to eradicate *nyakatsi* [thatch-roofed houses] from the country, part of Rwanda's Vision 2020 programme to transform itself into a middle-income economy by the year 2020.[2] Opposing this initiative, as I will show, had real-world consequences. While there is no actual political opposition in Rwanda, little freedom of speech, and with strict laws regulating what one is allowed to say, especially about the past, the genocide, and/or ethnicity,[3] music and popular culture provide 'moments of freedom'[4] where young people are able to articulate alternative 'visions' of their lives, looking to the past and the future in new – and very public – ways.

Yet 'Bye-bye *Nyakatsi*' must be read for more than its political content. It is also a source of pleasure and amusement for Rwandan music lovers, its lyrics a bizarre linguistic *mélange*. In this sense, I am interested in its 'social life',[5] how it is lived by fans and put to work in their everyday lives. After examining the song's politics and lyrics, I go on to consider a friend's use of 'Bye-bye *Nyakatsi*' to comment upon and commemorate an important event, capturing both the possibilities and anxieties of 'life change', as he put it. In this way, I suggest that rap and hip hop songs encourage debates about what it means to be Rwandan, and indirectly challenge the 'fast-forward'[6] pace at which the country's development is taking place. As President Paul Kagame has recently declared, 'There is a view that development is a marathon, not a sprint. We do not agree. Development is a marathon that must be run at a sprint.'[7] Both forms of Bye-bye Nyakatsi – the song and the housing programme – raise difficult questions about social and cultural memory, and reveal how the state attempts to 'eradicate' its critics through processes of exclusion and silencing. The song, 'Bye-bye *Nyakatsi*', suggests that one of the ways marginalized young people in Rwanda respond to this is through the defiant posturing of hip hop and the ironic performance of 'swagga'.

While I explore a few of the song's resonances here, it is with the acknowledgment always that my reading is provisional. Like any good song, 'Bye-bye *Nyakatsi*' escapes any one interpretation. Instead, it takes on new meanings with each listen as fans recreate it to speak to and make sense of their lives and their relationships – with themselves, with others, and with their country.

## The politics of Bye-Bye Nyakatsi: 'Some of them just do not want to change'

Before turning to the lyrics of 'Bye-bye *Nyakatsi*', I first consider the government's Bye-bye Nyakatsi programme. Inaugurated in 2008, the state housing project, also called Guca Nyakatsi, aimed to eradicate traditional thatch-roofed houses from the country in an effort to support 'national social economic development'.[8] The project, run by the Ministry of Local Government (MINALOC), the Rwandan Defence Forces (RDF), and the Rwanda National Police (RNP), was one aspect of the larger Vision 2020 programme, which 'aspires for Rwanda to become a modern, strong and a united nation, proud of its fundamental values, politically stable and without discrimination amongst its citizens'; it aimed, as noted above, to transform the country into a middle-income economy by 2020.[9] More specifically, Guca Nyakatsi contributed to a nationwide effort to reorganize communities, traditionally composed of rural homesteads scattered across hillsides, into clearly defined administrative units [*imidugudu*] that would allow for easier access to infrastructure, healthcare, and education. To some, however, this forced villagization, which was introduced in 1996 as a way to safeguard national security, was yet another way the authoritarian Rwandan state, led by Kagame's Rwandan Patriotic Front (RPF), was enacting an aggressive 'social engineering' programme to 'modernize, rationalize, and control the countryside'.[10] The *imidugudu* policy paid little attention to the histories, practices, and desires of the local population and, to some critics, ultimately 'reinforced social tensions around land, often along ethnic lines'.[11]

Although the Bye-bye Nyakatsi programme was part of the *imidugudu* project, it had its own goals. A MINALOC document outlined three in particular: 'Support national development'; 'Improve community policing and Civil Military Cooperation (CIMIC)'; and 'Improve rural social-economic transformation'.[12] Perceived by Rwanda's forward-looking authorities as fire and health hazards, *nyakatsi* were condemned as symbols of poverty – despite the fact that they also provided effective protection from the elements, and thatched roofs were much less noisy than tin ones when it rained.[13] The programme began by identifying Rwandans living in *nyakatsi* and categorizing them into three groups according to their poverty level and 'attitude'; a sensitization campaign followed espousing the virtues of 'decent housing'; and, finally, a joint operation force was created in January 2011 to assist families with their resettlement, with a deadline of May 2011.[14] Rwandans in the diaspora contributed to their own Bye-bye Nyakatsi project, and private companies, international NGOs, and development agencies followed suit.[15] With a budget of Rwf4 billion, the Bye-bye Nyakatsi programme ultimately succeeded in moving 124,671 families out of *nyakatsi* and into 'decent houses'.[16]

The implementation of the policy attracted a healthy dose of controversy. In some areas it was employed too swiftly and *nyakatsi* were destroyed before replacement housing could be built.[17] In one example, local officials in Bugesera pulled down the thatch-roofed house of a couple with nine children before they had provided alternative accommodation. The local leader who supervised the destruction of the family's home reportedly stated that 'it would be better for them to sleep in the bushes than go on living in nyakatsi' – which is exactly what the family was forced to do.[18] In Musanze, residents complained that their *nyakatsi* were destroyed before the government supplied them with corrugated iron sheets.[19] Augustin Kampayana, the official in charge of the Bye-bye Nyakatsi project, was unapologetic. '[T]he people were sensitized long enough,' he was quoted as saying. 'They knew well in advance that they had to save money to buy iron sheets and to have bricks made, so for anyone to still be in *nyakatsi* up to now only means that it is in their general attitudes to prefer to live in grass thatched houses. Some of them just do not want to change, but we cannot let these drag everyone else back.'[20] To the government, there were enough poverty alleviation schemes in place for the poor to help themselves. Those who did not participate in the project simply did not have the correct 'attitudes'.[21]

The Bye-bye Nyakatsi policy was also criticized for disproportionately targeting the Batwa, Rwanda's 'pygmy' community and one of the most marginalized groups in the country. In March 2011, the Unrepresented Nations and Peoples Organization (UNPO) briefed the UN Committee on the Elimination of Racial Discrimination on the difficulties facing the Batwa, pointing out that the policy had left hundreds of Batwa families homeless during the rainy season.[22] The following month, Survival International rallied its supporters to tweet the Rwandan government (@RwandaGov) to 'reconsider their campaign'.[23] After receiving hundreds of tweets, Kampayana admitted that occasionally the government did use force implementing the policy.[24]

Yet, in June 2011, when UNPO – in coordination with the Society for Threatened Peoples (STP) – raised concerns about the 'speed' at which the Bye-bye Nyakatsi programme was being implemented at the UN Human Rights Council, a Rwandan official dismissed the criticism.[25] In his closing remarks at the session, the Minister of Justice and Attorney General of Rwanda, Tharcisse Karugarama, accused the UNPO and other NGOs of making statements that were 'careless and do not reflect the reality on the ground'.[26]

Within Rwanda, criticizing the Bye-bye Nyakatsi policy came at a much higher price. During his Christmas sermon in December 2010, Abbé Emile Nsengiyumva, a Catholic priest at the parish of Karenge in eastern Rwanda, spoke out against the housing programme and the government's proposed restrictions on family planning. According to one Catholic priest I knew who was familiar with the case, Nsengiyumva had critiqued the destruction of *nyakatsi* at night, and the use of contraceptive pills and abortion. After the sermon, Nsengiyumva was arrested and charged with 'endangering state security and inciting civil disobedience'.[27] In July 2011, a court in Rwamagana sentenced him to 18 months in prison.[28] Priests were not the only ones punished. In July 2012, five local leaders from Nyagatare District were suspended because they 'allegedly lied to their superiors that eradication of thatched houses had been successfully done'.[29]

It was into this contentious political context that the song, 'Bye-bye Nyakatsi', was released in the summer of 2012. Bulldogg, who began his music career while still at high school in Kigali in 2006, was known as a rapper who tackled important social issues. A recent profile on a popular

Kinyarwanda-language website described him as 'an outspoken artist' who 'speaks his mind on problems in the Rwandan music industry such as injustice and inequality'.[30] His fans never tired of telling me how he was 'good in Kinyarwanda', and one of the smartest rappers in the game [*agakino*]. Born and raised in Kigali, he had studied for a time at the National University of Rwanda in Butare, and was studying literature at the Kigali Institute of Education (KIE) during my fieldwork.

### 'I can't have a good life ... if I still live in *nyakatsi*'

With its catchy chorus mixing English and Kinyarwanda, its pounding piano rhythm, haunting guitar melody, and increasingly frantic rap rifting, it's perhaps not surprising that 'Bye-bye *Nyakatsi*' became a favourite among Rwanda's ever-growing hip hop fan base. Over the course of my fieldwork, I saw Bulldogg perform the song dozens of times – both in front of thousands of fans and in front of a handful – always to wild applause and laughter. I discuss the lyrics below, but with an important caveat. Since Bulldogg raps so quickly and uses such dense Kinyarwanda, what follows is a *working* translation, by no means definitive. In an attempt to appreciate the 'poetry' of the lyrics, as a friend who helped me translate the song put it, the following version is interpretive rather than literal. 'The way he wrote the song is complicated and even Rwandese who are addicted to [entertainment news] cannot get the real sense of it', my friend explained. 'The style of writing is complex – it depends on the listener to get the meaning.' Rather than lament my failure to pin down its meaning, therefore, I want to emphasize the song's linguistic and semantic slipperiness. A large part of its appeal – and of Kinyarwanda rap and hip hop songs generally – is exactly this ability to 'hide' messages. As one devoted fan made clear to me, 'Rap is a mixture, it's the art of combination of life, wisdom, hiding messages somewhere so people can try to come and be interested in what you are saying and ask you what you want to mean.' In this way, rap constantly creates and recreates its own community.

### 'Bye-bye *Nyakatsi*' by Bulldogg[31]

'Bye-bye *Nyakatsi*' begins with Bulldogg introducing himself to the listener, listing a number of his aliases (El Patron, Buddha, the chameleon's eye, etc.), before the chorus, sung by a female artist named Gloria, kicks off.[32] Gloria sings the lines of the chorus, in between which Bulldogg raps the alternate lines that I indicate below in brackets. Three verses then ensue, each followed by the same chorus.

**Chorus:** I can't have a good life, no I can't
(If I still live in *nyakatsi*)
I've got my bags ready, I've got to go, that's the way it is
(*Bye-bye nyakatsi!*)
Be easy on me, guide me, hold me, don't let me go, help me get far

**Verse 1:** Life: wars, money, [it's] a problem
*Illuminati*: the devil, riches, sacrifices
Family: offspring, inheritance, siblings, tribulations, poisoning, [that's]
    the new Kigali, *hahaha!*
Resist: provoke
Work hard: hustle, be alert, tie up your *kimono*, do your *kata*, sleep tight
Look good: take a picture, send it to your mother so she doesn't forget
The Creator: blesses who he pleases, *ok, ok!*
Get on top: create misbalance, eat greens, feed whom you please; greed,
    selfishness
Buddha: dodge, *fraude*, *faux papiers, police*: corruption
*Infirmière: fénéante*, let patients die

**Chorus**

**Verse 2:** *Technologie*, progress, *Facebook*: chat
New *vision*: change, new fashion, Lord almighty, a virus
A journey: SAR IK 4, *Come Again, entretien*[33]
*Déception, ohlala! Fuck me good*
Oh I had gone astray, guide me, help me
*Rastafari, El Patron, peace and love*
Get a drink but be wise, man up
Hit a woman: no, that's taboo nowadays, 'Let her leave, I'll be fine'
Rwanda, *swagga*, Kigali, the capital
No haters, no bitches, *Customer care, oh yeah!*

**Chorus**

**Verse 3:** The sunrise brings serenity and growth in Gisaka
But the sunset takes away the yields in a basket to Kinyaga
In Rwanda we focus more on making money
We play *inanga*[34] so good that our skills raise the eyebrows of the
    mighty ones
And the sound reminds them that our issues don't bring food to the

table

So they dig deep like surgeons looking for a way towards business
partnerships

They hire agents to spy for them so they know who's hunting them
down

And when they know their enemy, they strengthen their grudge

I move forward without caring what people say

Without caring about the people who say it

So I can aim at one thing: increase my productivity

My only taste is my country

*Chorus*

## The song in three aspects

'Bye-bye *Nyakatsi*'s cryptic verses, creative wordplay, and humorous, even
playful, tone, defy any easy interpretation. Here, I explore three aspects of
the song, and make no claims that my reading answers Bulldogg's
intentions. Given Rwanda's political climate, I am in no way associating
Bulldogg with the following discussion. Rather, I am more interested in
the possibilities for interpretation that the song opens up.

Firstly I want to consider the contrast between the apparent hopefulness
of the chorus – 'I can't have a good life … /(If I still live in *nyakatsi*)' –
and the aggressive onslaught of the verses. In the first verse in particular,
the speaker reels off all the negative attributes of social life in present-day
Rwanda and the 'new Kigali': war, money, Illuminati, the devil, poisoning,
fraud, fake documents, corruption, greed, selfishness – the list goes on.
The juxtaposition undermines the cheeriness of the chorus, confronted
as it is by the harsh reality of the city. Has leaving *nyakatsi* really led to a
'good life'? Yet the 'new vision' allows for new possibilities. The city is
equally the home of money, riches, family, technology, Facebook, change,
and new fashion. New identities can be created and assumed. One can
become a Rastafari and spread peace and love; or, like Bulldogg, one can
refashion oneself into a figure of authority and power (Buddha, El Patron).
As my friend who helped translate the song put it, 'The chorus talks about
*nyakatsi* but listening to the whole song it's more of a metaphor of just a
bad life, rather than a [type of] house – a person moving away, who is
seeking for better.'

Secondly, the song can be read as a set of directives. In this sense, it is a
*mode d'emploi*, an instruction manual on how to navigate the treacherous
terrain of the city. We must resist, provoke, work hard, hustle, fight, tie up

our *kimonos*, do our *katas*, take a photo, look good, create misbalance, eat greens, get a drink, man up, etc. We must respond to the deception of the city by aggressively resisting its traps. At the same time, the social world the song describes is one of regulations. Just as we must say goodbye to *nyakatsi*, so new policies govern relationships between people, particularly between men and women. This is captured in the line in the second verse, 'Hit a woman: no, that's taboo nowadays'. With the RPF's assumption of power, Rwanda's progressive gender policies have promoted women to unprecedented positions of leadership in the government, civil society, and the private sector. In the recent parliamentary election in September 2013, for example, women won 64 per cent of the seats, maintaining Rwanda's status as the country with the highest percentage of female parliamentarians in the world.[35] Yet for many Rwandan men, young and old, this promotion of women was seen as a zero-sum game, with men the eternal losers. Indeed, a man couldn't even beat his wife any more without getting into trouble. In misogynistic rhetoric, Bulldogg's lyric responds to this sense of change being imposed top-down, with no explanation and no possibility of discussion. This was 'the way it is', as the chorus says, and one had no choice but to accept it.

The next lines, however, point to a way out of this predicament by adopting a posture of ironic acquiescence. '"Let her leave, I'll be fine"/Rwanda, *swagga*, Kigali, the capital/No haters, no bitches [prostitutes], *Customer care, oh yeah!*', Bulldogg raps. Although the previous verse has described the city as one of moral compromise, even calamity, the speaker falls back on the official state discourse of Kigali as the model city, one of the 'safest and friendliest of African capitals'. As the City of Kigali's official website declares, 'Our vision is to make City of Kigali [*sic*] a safer, cleaner, and more competitive, modern city with expanding opportunity for sustainable development of its citizens and the country at large.'[36] It is exactly this 'official' image of Kigali that the song has previously worked so hard to deconstruct and invert. At this moment in the song, it's as if the speaker throws up his hands and says, 'This is not the way it really is, but I understand that I have to perform as if it were in order to survive.' This sense of ironic, even mocking, performance is suggested by the term 'swagga'. One fronts, one acts as though one is in control, projecting confidence, wealth, and power, even if one is socially and politically strait-jacketed.

This leads me to the third aspect of 'Bye-bye *Nyakatsi*' that I want to address. For all its aggressive, masculinist bravado – Bulldogg's rough voice all but barks out the lyrics – the song also intimates a desire for personal connection and relationships. There is an undercurrent of vulnerability. The final line of the chorus, after all, is, 'Be easy on me, guide me, hold me, don't let me go, help me get far.' In verse two the speaker exhorts, '*Fuck me good*/Oh I had gone astray, guide me, help me.' Amid the uncertainties of the city, he has lost his way and pleads for assistance. This sense of defiant vulnerability – even paranoia – comes across most clearly in the final verse. Not only does the speaker describe a world of social inequality – the yields of Gisaka are taken away to Kinyaga – but also of fear and intimidation. If one excels or rises above the status quo – by playing *inanga* too well – then the 'eyebrows of the mighty ones' are raised. The powerful have spies to help root out those who are 'hunting them down'. It is, in some ways, a description of a totalitarian regime where resistance is silenced and compliance is bought with the promise of money or 'business partnerships'. The humour of the first two verses has dropped away, replaced by a sense of urgency and violence: 'And when they know their enemy, they strengthen their grudge.' Yet, despite this dangerous social and political world, the speaker remains defiant. 'I move forward without caring what people say,' he raps. He will focus instead on his own 'productivity', on carving out a place for himself in *his* country. A country, the previous lines have suggested, that has no place for him; as a young, aggressive man, he is yet another form of *nyakatsi* that it is trying to 'eradicate'.

## A 'new beginning'

Although I have focused on the political implications of 'Bye-bye *Nyakatsi*' above, it is not my intention to reduce the significance of the song to its perceived politics. For Bulldogg's fans, the song resonated with them on a more personal level, offering a way to make sense of the rapid changes in their lives from a position of defiance and humour. As much as I take the song seriously, it is also extremely funny. Indeed, whenever Bulldogg performed it, audience members – young men and women alike – would often burst into laughter at its bizarre use of language, especially at the 'hit a woman' line. 'Bye-bye *Nyakatsi*' was also taken up by friends to commemorate important transitions in their everyday lives. When a friend of mine was given the opportunity to study in the US, he posted on Facebook upon arrival a photo which showed him wearing a black suit and tie posing in front of the American flag, and with the following caption: 'New beginning … with life change … bye bye nyakatsi … feeling like m excited.'

In this surprising and clever invocation of the song's title, my friend marked an important 'life change'. After a difficult childhood growing up as a genocide orphan, he hoped the move to America would bring new opportunities. Yet his goodbye was bittersweet. Just as Bulldogg's lyrics articulate the possibilities and dangers of modern urban life, its freedoms and constraints, so too did my friend's use of the borrowed phrase suggest both the gains and losses of migration. He had left Rwanda to further his studies, but he had also left behind the very community in which songs, such as 'Bye-bye *Nyakatsi*', circulate. The reaction of his friends to the photo on Facebook was mixed. While some exclaimed approvingly that he was now 'in the land of promise' ['*mu gihugu cy'isezerano!!!*'], others cautioned him, 'Hahahahaaa never forget your root (ur RWANDAN),' and 'Hahaha don't forget where u come from.'

While, according to the government, eradicating 'traditional' *nyakatsi* was a sign of the country's development and a key aspect of its Vision 2020 programme, *nyakatsi*, as physical objects, were also an important part of the country's material culture – and in some respects have remained so at present. *Nyakatsi* are Rwanda's 'iconic architecture' – the most visible example of which, after all, is the King's Palace in Nyanza – and many Rwandans, including the family of President Kagame, allegedly grew up in them.[37] In this way, *nyakatsi* can also be understood as sites of nostalgia, but, importantly, as sites of what I call a 'stubborn' or 'critical' nostalgia – a longing for a past Rwandans were and still are encouraged – even forced – to forget. I am in no way suggesting that Rwandans want to keep on living in *nyakatsi* or forego the benefits of 'development'. Rather I'm suggesting that this form of nostalgia is a way for them to critically engage with state discourses about development and modernity, a way to slow down for a moment and reflect upon what the country's rapid 'sprint' really means – and what and whom are being left behind in the process. It is, in a sense, a way to perform the 'labor of memory' or the 'critical use of memory', as Paul Ricoeur calls it, in a context where a difficult, even incomprehensible, past has become increasingly politicized.[38]

## Conclusion

By centring my discussion of popular music in Rwanda on 'Bye-bye *Nyakatsi*', I hope to demonstrate the importance of songs in structuring and giving meaning to young people's lives in Kigali and beyond. In a complex political, social, and moral context, a song like 'Bye-bye *Nyakatsi*' articulates the ambiguities and ambivalences inherent in post-genocide Rwandan social life, especially in the 'new Kigali', as Bulldogg calls it. Faced with these difficult circumstances, the song's speaker advocates defiance and the confident performance of 'swagga', and claims by these ploys, a place in a city and country that may not be comfortable with his presence. At the same time, by appropriating 'Bye-bye *Nyakatsi*' for their own ends, young Rwandans use the song to mark and celebrate important 'life changes', expressing both excitement and anxiety. 'Bye-bye *Nyakatsi*' is significant, I think, because it encourages listeners to reflect upon the country's 'sprint' towards development and the 'sacrifices' – of people, of culture, of memory – that are being made in its name. One of the key ways that Rwandans are interacting with their difficult history, I suggest, is through a form of 'critical' or 'stubborn' nostalgia – a longing for the past they are supposed to want to leave behind. Yet while the government seek to physically eradicate thatch-roofed houses from the country's landscape, the cultural significance of *nyakatsi* prevents them from disappearing entirely from the public's imagination. Rap and hip hop songs create 'moments of freedom' where this past can be kept present and alive.

'Bye-bye *Nyakatsi*' demonstrates the necessity of paying attention to popular culture in Rwanda. With their multiple resonances, humorous associations, and creative word-play, songs are important forms of social commentary and social memory – not to mention pleasure – for Rwandans and non-Rwandans alike. They are good to think with, and even better to listen to.

NOTES

I spent a total of 16 months in Rwanda. The main period of my fieldwork was from September 2011 to December 2012, followed by another month in September 2013. This research was funded by the Clarendon Scholarship-St Hugh's College Louey Scholarship, Canadian Centennial Scholarship Fund, Godfrey Lienhardt Memorial Fund, and the Barbinder Watson Fund.

1. Marc Sommer, *Stuck: Rwandan Youth and the Struggle for Adulthood* (Athens: U of Georgia P, 2012), p. 13.
2. For clarity's sake, 'Bye-bye *Nyakatsi*' refers to the song, while Bye-bye Nyakatsi refers to the government programme.
3. See Susan Thomson, *Whispering Truth to Power: Everyday Resistance to Reconciliation in Postgenocide Rwanda* (Madison: U of Wisconsin P, 2013); Andrea Purdeková, 'Civic Education and Social Transformation in Post-Genocide Rwanda: Forging the Perfect Development Subjects', in *Rwanda Fast Forward: Social, Economic, Military and Reconciliation Prospects*, eds, Maddalena Campioni and Patrick Noack (New York: Palgrave Macmillian, 2012), pp. 192-209; *Remaking Rwanda: State Building and Human Rights after Mass Violence*, eds, Scott Straus and Lars Waldorf (Madison: U of Wisconsin P, 2011); Helen M. Hintjens, 'Post-genocide Identity Politics in Rwanda', *Ethnicities*, 8 (2008) 5-41; Johan Pottier, *Re-Imagining Rwanda: Conflict, Survival and Disinformation in the Late Twentieth Century* (Cambridge: Cambridge UP, 2002).
4. Johannes Fabian, *Moments of Freedom: Anthropology and Popular Culture* (Charlottesville:

UP of Virginia, 1998). See also Karin Barber, 'Popular Arts in Africa', *African Studies Review*, 30 (1987) 1-78.

5. *The Social Life of Things: Commodities in Cultural Perspective*, ed., Arjun Appadurai (Cambridge: Cambridge UP, 1986).

6. *Rwanda Fast Forward*, eds, Campioni and Noack.

7. See <online.wsj.com/news/articles/SB10001424127887324767004578485234078 541160>

8. See <minaloc.gov.rw/fileadmin/documents/Minaloc_Documents/ToRs%20Nyakatsi %20eradication%20signed%20dec%202010.pdf>

9. See <minaloc.gov.rw/fileadmin/documents/Minaloc_Documents/ToRs%20Nyakatsi %20eradication%20signed%20dec%202010.pdf>

10. Scott Straus and Lars Waldorf, 'Introduction: Seeing Like a Post-Conflict State', in *Remaking Rwanda*, eds, Straus and Waldorf, pp. 3-21.

11. Catharine Newbury, 'High Modernism at the Ground Level: The *Imidugudu* Policy in Rwanda', in *Remaking Rwanda,* eds, Straus and Waldorf , pp. 223-9 (p. 235). See also Alison Des Forges, 'Land in Rwanda: Winnowing Out the Chaff', in *L'Afrique des Grands Lacs: Annuaire 2005-2006*, eds, Filip Reyntjens and Stefaan Marysse (Paris: L'Harmattan, 2006), pp. 353-71.

12. See <minaloc.gov.rw/fileadmin/documents/Minaloc_Documents/ToRs%20Nyakatsi %20eradication%20signed%20dec%202010.pdf>

13. Simon Turner, 'Staging the Rwandan Diaspora: The Politics of Performance', *African Studies*, 72 (2013), 265-84 (p. 268).

14. See <independent.co.ug/News/regional-news/4088-operation-bye-bye-huts>; and <focus.rw/wp/2011/05/nyakatsi-eradication-moves-125000-people-into-decent-housing/>

15. See <independent.co.ug/News/regional-news/4088-operation-bye-bye-huts>

16. See <minaloc.gov.rw/fileadmin/documents/Minaloc_Documents/PROGRESS_ MADE_AND_MAIN_ACHIEVEMENTS_REGISTERED_FROM_2009_TO _2013_RSTF.pdf>

17. See <focus.rw/wp/2011/01/trials-and-tribulations-in-nyakatsi/>

18. See <focus.rw/wp/2011/01/trials-and-tribulations-in-nyakatsi/>

19. See <focus.rw/wp/2010/12/grass-thatched-houses-demolition-continues-despite-complaints/>

20. See <focus.rw/wp/2011/01/trials-and-tribulations-in-nyakatsi/>

21. Turner, 'Staging the Rwandan Diaspora'; also Purdeková, 'Civic Education and Social Transformation'.

22. See <unpo.org/article/12343>

23. See <survivalinternational.org/news/7154>

24. See <survivalinternational.org/news/7303>

25. See <unpo.org/article/12744>

26. See <unpo.org/article/12744>

27. See <hrw.org/world-report-2012/world-report-2012-rwanda>

28. See <freedomhouse.org/report/freedom-world/2012/rwanda>

29. See <newtimes.co.rw/news/index.php?a=56243&i=15062>

30. See <igihe.com/imyidagaduro/muzika/abahanzi/article/icyo-bamwe-mu-bahanzi-nyarwanda>

31. This translation must be credited to the brilliant and inspired work of a close friend who preferred not to be named. I had been working with an earlier translation of the song but it was 'too direct', as my friend, who is also a poet, pointed out. The poetry, humour, and playfulness of the song had been lost. My friend consulted a number of

friends to make sense of some of Bulldogg's more cryptic lyrics, so the translation should be considered a collaborative endeavour. In my view, this translation is a work of art in its own right, and I remain indebted to this friend. All the notes that accompany the song should be attributed to this friend as well. I italicize words of the song that were originally in English, French, or Japanese.

32. Bulldogg boasts of having more than 30 names. Notable names in English included Notorious, Motherboard, Database, Undertaker, and Viper.

33. SAR IK 4 is the address of the popular Kigali restaurant, Come Again. The image is of people, compared to cars, going to the restaurant for 'maintenance'.

34. *Inanga* is a traditional Rwandan instrument also known as a trough-zither.

35. See <gov.rw/Women-win-64-of-seats-in-parliamentary-elections-maintaining-number-one-spot-worldwide>

36. See <kigalicity.gov.rw/spip.php?article109>

37. See <independent.co.ug/News/regional-news/4088-operation-bye-bye-huts>

38. Quoted in René Lemarchand, 'The Politics of Memory in Post-Genocide Rwanda', in *After Genocide: Transitional Justice, Post-Conflict Reconstruction and Reconciliation in Rwanda and Beyond*, eds, Phil Clark and Zachary D. Kaufman (London: Hurst & Company, 2008), pp. 65-76.

HO JIA XUAN & REBECCA LIM

# An interview with Tash Aw

Shifting between seemingly disparate narratives, Tash Aw's latest work, *Five-Star Billionaire* (2013), traces the lives of five Malaysians in Shanghai, all of whom share a common goal: to fulfil their material desires one way or another owing to an almost desperate fascination with the notion of success, with having, in the words of one of the characters, 'made it'. His two other novels to date are *The Harmony Silk Factory* (2005) and *Map of the Invisible World* (2009).

Tash Aw is currently one of the most successful of Malaysian writers. He won the Whitbread Book Awards for First Novel Award, as well as the Commonwealth Writers Prize for Best First Novel (Asia Pacific Region). *The Harmony Silk Factory* was shortlisted for the Man Booker Prize in 2005.

Born in Taipei, Tash Aw grew up in Kuala Lumpur, Malaysia, and moved to London in his teenage years. He studied law at the University of Cambridge and University of Warwick, before embarking upon a career as a novelist. He is currently a resident writer at Nanyang Technological University, Singapore, and part of NTU's Creative Writing programme.

*Rebecca Lim*: Hi, Tash, you've been away from home (Malaysia) for quite some time. Can you tell us how this distance has affected your perspective on life?

*Tash Aw*: When you move away from home, you get a clearer perspective of yourself and your country, and your sense of who you are changes. When you stay at home and are completely surrounded by a familiar environment with people whom you've known since forever, you lose a sense of how different you are from them, and you then presume a lot of homogeneity. In Malaysia, I get swallowed up by family matters, by politics, by going out with friends, and it becomes difficult to see if problems – whether they exist at a domestic or national level – are actually real problems or if they are not such a big deal.

Also when you come from a fundamentally quite messed-up country, like Malaysia, there is this sense that people who live there permanently have to just survive it, and the only way you can survive it is by becoming slightly immune to how abnormal the situation is. It is only when you go away that you say, 'hang on, this is really not how it should be'. And so, I think that being away from home is the only way you can get that perspective, and it has definitely changed the way I see myself and where I'm from. So that's one of the main advantages of being away from home, because it gives you clarity as a writer. But my family is still there, so when I go back, I don't feel divorced from the place. I have enough of a distance to view the country and its problems objectively, and I think objectivity is a fundamental thing in writing, especially regarding emotions.

**RL:** Based on what you've said – that being away has given you more awareness and a different perspective – was any of that a key impulse behind your intention to situate such a large part of the events in your novels within Malaysia?

**TA:** Not really. As a writer, you can only write about what is most fundamental to your state of being. And I think that where you are from is the most important thing. For most people, as for myself, questions of race and identity and belonging are very fundamental. Obviously I can't write about migration from the perspective of Bangladesh or America because I've never experienced it, and I wouldn't feel emotionally connected to that experience, whereas I do feel emotionally connected to Malaysia. My writing has something at stake when I write about those issues.

**RL:** Let's relate that to an essential question of identity and belonging that a lot of minorities in Malaysia have to grapple with. You've mentioned in other interviews that you feel both an insider and outsider in Malaysia. A lot of people share that sentiment. Are you familiar with Yasmin Ahmad's work? In her film *Gubra*, one of the characters, Alan, says that being a Chinese Malaysian is like being in love with someone who doesn't love you back, and that is how he situates his relationship with Malaysia. I was just wondering, how do your novels help you figure out Malaysia, or how do they help situate your relationship with Malaysia?

**TA:** The process of writing my novels took a long time, at least four or five years each. Obviously during this time you change as a person, and you change as a writer. My feelings about Malaysia are muddy, but the things I become clearer on are feelings that will always be unresolved. I think Malaysia is a country that is born out of very mixed circumstances. For one thing, its people come from so many different parts of the world, and necessarily this is going to produce a culture that is quite mixed up, in good ways as well as bad ways. People talk a lot about hybridity, which I think is an over-used phrase. But I think the by-product of hybridity is messiness, and messiness is a good thing, because it is a constantly evolving thing. It means that you can't settle on any one clear emotional response to that thing.

And I think that is what is interesting about Malaysia, and interesting about life in general, that things keep changing. I am very suspicious of people who have one set view on one particular culture which never changes, because anything that is worth grappling with is going to change, is going to be complex.

**Ho Jia Xuan:** We've noticed that all your novels have ambiguous endings. Is it because, as you said, these issues cannot be resolved, or are you deliberately trying to retain narrative possibilities?

**TA:** Yes, exactly. Growing up in these circumstances means that I don't really have a fixed view of things; I don't have a judgement on things. It's very hard to be judgemental. I mean, I do have firm views on some things, but there are other things I don't have firm views on. And to summarize the lives of Malaysian people, or the lives of people in general, in a neat way, seems to be the very antithesis of what fiction should be. Fiction should be about exploring and posing questions rather than reaching very firm judgements. And I think in many ways my novels reflect that evolving nature of Malaysian lives, that they are still in flux, and you can see very big changes looming, especially with the upcoming elections [May 2013].

I spent at least half of my life growing up in very fixed circumstances, where institutionalized divisions really looked set to remain. The fact that these may just go overnight means that even the things you most take for granted are up for change. I like the sense of lives being in flux, lives being capable of evolution. And personally I love novels that give the impression the characters live on at the end of the narrative, that their lives don't finish there and then.

**RL:** Can we ask you a question about your process of writing? You say that your novels do resolve in some ways, but the conclusions are not very clear. At what point in the writing process do you know when to end your novels or get a sense that you've written enough?

**TA:** That's a million-dollar question. But I think that basically with novel writing, it's a balancing act between very deliberate decisions on the one hand, and, on the other, allowing the natural progression of the characters to dictate the plot. Emotionally, one figures out the connection with one's novel, but it also has to be an intellectual process. I think novel writing is about the intellect as much as it is about emotions, and the two have to meet in some way. To me, the best novels are the ones with endings that provoke thought, which is why I find Hollywood-like endings very unsatisfying, because you can anticipate the way it will pan out in a formulaic way. It may give you a temporary boost like when you eat cheap chocolate, but after five minutes you don't feel nourished by it, you don't go away thinking about it.

**HJX:** Do you consciously experiment with the workings of time in your novels?

**TA:** Yeah, I do. I'm interested in how time works, how people remember things, and I think it's particularly relevant in a lot of Asian cultures, which have a very uneasy relationship with their recent past. We either like to look at ourselves like we're countries rooted very far in the past, or else very modern, with nothing in between. A lot of it has to do with the fact that, for people in the twentieth and twenty-first centuries, it is often very difficult, very painful, to remember the past. I am very aware that people of my generation have this deliberately blurred view of what went on in their parents' generation.

**HJX:** Especially in *Map of the Invisible World*, you tend to play around with the verb tenses and shift the narratives across different time frames.

**TA:** Yes, and this becomes more pronounced in *Five-Star Billionaire*. I think we often read a novel with the expectation that all the characters should be advancing at the same time. But people start off their lives at different points, and when their lives happen to intersect, you might get references to scenes that have already happened in someone else's life. Then you see these miniscule gaps in time that make you rethink your own position with regard to time and evolution. I believe people also experience time differently and I definitely get the sense, when I travel between Europe and Asia, that things are speeded up a lot, and there is this constant code of looking forward in Asia, whereas in the West ... I won't say that it is backward looking, but there is certainly a greater attachment to the past. And I think that attachment has the effect of tying time down. So, yeah, I do like to experiment with notions of time, and how that affects the concept of one's self in relation to others.

**RL:** I find it interesting that, while you say we Asians seem to be generally looking forward, your first two novels involve the act of looking back into history and the characters' pasts. Do you think that as a novelist you have a responsibility to retrieve these stories?

**TA:** As a novelist in my situation, yeah, I do. When I wrote those novels, it really felt that all those stories weren't just about preserving things in the past, they were also about wanting to relate to how people live today. For example, the whole idea of how we deal with our guilt and shame by not talking about it, and by the need to reinvent ourselves. So I think the way I handled this was to explore the cult of reinvention in Asia.

You see, many of these Chinese tycoons, they actually commission writers to write a history about themselves that often conforms to this overly simplistic Hollywood arc where you have humble beginnings and then you become rich. But they don't talk about what they had to go through to get to where they're at, because a lot of it involves quite painful and sometimes quite shameful events that go back to the Second World War and the Japanese occupation. A lot of racial divisions in Malaysia, though not the same as they are now, became escalated during the war. Look, for example, at the Chinese who live in the rural areas of Malaysia, they are associated still with the communist movement. So, you know, all those films like *The Last Communist* made people feel some comfort. It was a searching film, not what I would call a subversive film, but a film that basically asked questions that needed to be asked, to embrace stories and people's points of view. And I was trying to do that in a slightly different context in my novels. So for me it wasn't necessarily an obsession with the past.

**RL:** But do you have any questions in your head that fit the image that you want the readers to get? Do you want to leave them with some impression of Malaysia that you want them to have? What are some questions you want the Malaysians in particular to think about when they read your novels?

**TA:** I guess, if we are talking specifically about Malaysian readers, you need to ask questions about how they live, about whether or not the choices that have been handed down to them by family or society are actually the ones they want, rather than the ones they think are inevitable, because there is a sense that, since we have to live in the middle of a big society, we unconsciously ingest the desire and the ambitions and the aspirations of that society. Going back to the original question, that is another reason why going away from home can sometimes be a useful thing, even though it can be quite scary from a logical point of view, because it can give clarity as to what you really want to do in your life. I don't know if people actually get that when they read my works, and in a sense it's not really important to me. I think what it is is that they read the novels and engage with them emotionally. In other words, I am very hesitant to be prescriptive as a writer, my main aim is that I'm a storyteller who captures stories that are around me, and every book is different because I have a different aim with every book.

*HJX:* The settings of your first two novels were post-independent countries, but the third novel makes a huge leap to the fast-paced and urbanized setting of Shanghai. Was there any intention in locating your characters in such a setting? Was there a kind of effect you wanted to achieve?

*TA:* I think there is in so many Asian societies – and this is probably more pronounced in Singapore than Malaysia – a concern with modernity. That's why many Singaporeans and Malaysians are so drawn to China. It represents an expression of high-octane modernity on the surface. So I guess I wanted to see how people would react in those circumstances. It made sense that I dealt with these themes, but the original intention was more in connection with broad themes like migration and mobility, and just came from my personal experience of travelling around, living in Shanghai, and seeing and meeting Malaysians and Singaporeans. I find it interesting and a little ironic that our grandfathers and great-grandfathers had come from China to Southeast Asia, but we are doing the reverse – the difference is that the first wave of migration came out of people having no choice, while this new wave was totally out of choice. Except that when you talk about choice, some people have more than others, and that is written in the book.

I can say the novel was a grand project to map the whole history of Malaysia in the last eighty years. As a writer, you can have these huge ambitions yet, when you get down to writing, it often doesn't work. So, ultimately, you can only really write what you can write. You know, I always have this vague idea that I need to examine how we, as a people, have lived, so the first novel in the way I see it now is really about my grandparents, the second is about my parents' generation – though all the anxieties are not just specifically about them, but the anxieties the nation has felt over that time, during that time – and this recent novel is really concerned with my generation. All of which could mean that I don't really know where to go next! I mean it feels like my works so far have been playing catch-up, recording the unrecorded, and it is very important for me to represent an image of Malaysia that hasn't been seen in literature before.

*RL:* What are some of the literary influences which made you want to be a storyteller?

*TA:* A lot of the American novelists, such as Faulkner, who in particular has a way of being able to connect very deeply with a setting that is local to him. And to make it completely familiar yet fascinating to anyone who reads the novel. So Faulkner and Steinbeck as well, and *Moby Dick* and Melville in general, have made very strong impressions on me. As for prose style, I guess, there is Flaubert; and I like the way Nabokov deals with language, how he uses what is really his second language in a way that is unique to him, and that, I think, has influenced in a lot of ways how I work. I also read Chinese writers, some of whom are not necessarily very translatable.

*HJX:* Like Li Zi Shu?

*TA:*   Yeah, Li Zi Shu is one of the younger writers. Then there's Wang Anyi. I completely love her, and the way she writes about Shanghai in *The Song of Everlasting Sorrow* (2008). So I have very mixed tastes, but I guess the early influences were the American writers. Because I think there is among them a great sense of liberation. Writers write, and although the ones I've mentioned were operating in their first language, there was nonetheless an appropriating of form that was slightly new to them. Because the novel is really a European form, and by the time even of someone like Mark Twain, he was having to reinvent the novel in a local way, to set the template for generations of Americans to come. I guess that sense of pioneering novel writing spoke quite strongly to me.

*RL:*   So based on what you've said about these writers and the novel form, how would you say you yourself have grappled with the form of the novel?

*TA:*   Well, I play with the expectations, and we know how difficult it is for writers to deal with something completely new. Everyone writes out of a certain context and I write out of the context that is Malaysia. And my work has to be seen in the context also of performing. There is always the expectation that Southeast Asian novels look and work in a certain way, and the expectation is so strong even among people in Malaysia and Singapore. For example, when you deal with certain historical narratives, there is the expectation that they have to be very lush and exotic, and full of a certain beauty that is attached to the local landscape. And a certain kind of gorgeous suffering. To call it exoticization is too simplistic, it's more than that. It's different from that and also more than that. And I guess a part of my aim in writing the first novel was to subvert a lot of these expectations. I wanted to write a novel that makes people think it's about the Second World War but actually, when they read it, it wasn't giving them exactly what they wanted.

The second novel is really quite gritty and quite messy, and the third novel is totally open. Some people I sent copies to in England when the recent book came out said they found it very depressing. To me it is quite the opposite; I found *Five-Star Billionaire* quite an uplifting novel. But precisely because it does not make any judgement on the characters and how they are living. I suppose the reason those readers I mentioned said it was depressing was that Asia, they found, is actually very much concerned with all the stuff the West is concerned with, things like celebrity culture, materialism, urbanization, the nitty-gritty of going down to the shops and buying your instant noodles and crap meals. They found that very depressing because that is just what the West is like, and I think they had the expectation that Asia should give them something the West has lost. When you look at colonial history, Orientalism is something that has existed for a very long time, the notion that Asia supplies the West with a kind of innocence the West does not have. This is why certain cultures like Tibet appeal so strongly to the Western imagination. They represent a kind of purity and spirituality that the West believes it has lost. The West doesn't really want to see that Asia in many ways is just the same as the West.

Asia is obviously very different, but it's also the same in its difference, and I think that is what a lot of my work is concerned with. While they are very different countries and really different cultures, the parallels that exist between China and America are unmistakeable. So I guess my work, if I had to condense it to one thing, is about its concern with translating my own experiences about what it means to be Asian in a way that speaks equally to everyone.

*HJX:* So, in that case, judging by the way the novels have progressed in terms of setting, I'm assuming that the next novel will take place somewhere in London.

*TA:* No, no! I haven't decided, but I don't think that it's going to be a London novel. Which is not to say that London might not appear in the novel. In fact I already have, in the past, set scenes in London. But I have quite a straightforward relationship with London whereas my relationship with Malaysia is much more complicated. I don't know what it says about that relationship, but I guess it must signify that the place you grow up in is so emotional, and, however far you travel, it's a place that really interests you.

## SUCHEN CHRISTINE LIM
### THE RIVER'S SONG
Twickenham, UK: Aurora Metro 2013
ISBN: 9 781906 582982  pb  306pp  £9.99

By charting in parallel the fate of the Singapore River and the lives of the characters that depend on the river, Suchen Christine Lim's latest novel, *The River's Song*, grapples adeptly with concepts of national and personal identities. Interestingly, Lim does not portray her protagonist, Ping, as actively in search of an identity in this coming-of-age novel; instead, the author alludes to the character's longing for an identity by skilfully depriving Ping throughout most of the novel of definitive roles such as daughter, sister, wife or mother. That Ping comes to realize who she is, after a journey which takes her from Singapore to the United States, and back again, is rendered through her devotion to the pipa which carries the song of a heart that has never left home.

Lim's depictions of Ping's involuntary relocations as a child, and the damaging uprooting of those who are evicted from the riverbanks, poignantly accentuate, on a personal and a national level, the people's resistance and their sense of helplessness as they struggle with the city-state's rapidly changing landscape. The vividly depicted contrast between the development of the area around the river into business districts and the uprooted inhabitants who become unemployed desolates trapped in their HDB flats contributes further to a quietly accusatory tone in the novel. The characters' sense of belonging is movingly portrayed as a natural attachment to the river over years of living by its side, an attachment that is forcibly severed when the eviction notices arrive at their doors in the name of economic development and social progress. Crucially, the novel provokes the reader to wonder if such attachments associated with sites like the depicted Singapore River could be a potential germinating ground of an enduring national identity.

As the novel progresses, however, it becomes evident that, despite the striking portrayal of the characters' resistance to change, the author also recognizes the necessity and inevitability of change. Ultimately, the novel is an invitation to the reader to consider the difference between changes that are enforced by callous contrivance and changes that can be brought about through dialogue and compromise.

Music features prominently throughout the pages of the novel alongside the dazzling mix of languages – several Chinese dialects, Mandarin, Malay, Singlish and English. In addition to evoking the characters' poignant sense of longing, the music expertly realized by Lim is a language that connects the characters to one another. At this point, it is worth noting that Lim has sought to capture in romanized form the vibrancy of a number of the non-alphabetic languages that are spoken in Singapore, without neglecting to weave explanations of these romanized terms into her prose for an international reader. Although certain transitions between these terms and their explanations could be smoother, a reader who is familiar with these dialects and non-English languages in the novel will recognize that Lim's English translations of these words and expressions are impeccable, and a reader who does not know any of these languages can feel confident that she is not left clueless or excluded from the narrative.

Notably, towards the last few chapters of the novel, Singapore is described as a 'golden cage' and Weng, the male protagonist, is portrayed as determined to remain in Singapore despite his disapproval of the island state's restrictive politics. Three significant lines in the novel sum up his reason for staying: 'His flame will die if he doesn't leave. But if he does leave, it will affect his music, which is born out of this gilded cage. Out of this constant tension and contradiction in the city, and in him.' I interpret the lines to mean that, in the physical confines of the well-oiled city-state, Weng's political voice against social injustices may be silenced, but his deep-rooted allegiance to his personal and collective social memory expressed through music cannot be muted. In other words, the devotion to the well-being of one's home and community is more important than any methodically constructed and limiting definitions of a specific national identity.

Compared with her earlier novel, *A Fistful of Colours* (1992), which also explored issues of identity and belonging, Lim's astute treatment of these themes in *The River's Song* is indicative of her ongoing and mature search for answers to the question of what it could mean to be Singaporean.

H L Michelle Chiang, University of Leeds

# Notes on Contributors

**Mildred Barya** is a Ugandan writer and poet. She has published three volumes of poetry, *Men Love Chocolates But They Don't Say* (2002), *The Price of Memory: After the Tsunami* (2006), and *Give Me Room To Move My Feet* (2009) as well as numerous short stories. In 2008 she won the Pan African Literary Forum Prize for Africana Fiction.

**Elleke Boehmer** is Professor of World Literature in English at the University of Oxford. She has published *Colonial and Postcolonial Literature* (1995, 2005), *Empire, the National and the Postcolonial, 1890-1920* (2002), *Stories of Women* (2005), and *Nelson Mandela* (2008). She is the author of four acclaimed novels, including *Screens against the Sky* (short-listed David Hyam Prize, 1990), *Bloodlines* (shortlisted SANLAM prize), and *Nile Baby* (2008), and the short-story collection *Sharmilla and Other Portraits* (2010). A book on 'Empire's Networks' and a new novel, *The Shouting in the Dark*, are forthcoming.

**Eunice S. Ferreira** is Assistant Professor of Theatre at Skidmore College, New York. She is a director, choreographer, and academic. Her dissertation, *Theatre in Cape Verde: Resisting, Reclaiming, and Recreating National and Cultural Identity in Postcolonial Lusophone Africa*, examines post-independence theatre in Cape Verde from 1975 to 2005.

**Andrea Grant** is a Clarendon Scholar and D. Phil student in Social Anthropology at the University of Oxford. She is writing on religion and popular culture in Rwanda.

**Ho Jia Xuan** recently completed his MA at the Division of English, Nanyang Technological University, Singapore. His work in progress is in modernist fiction, critical theory, experimental writing, and, in particular, time as metaphor.

**Susan Kiguli** is Head of the Department of Literature at Makerere University, Uganda. She is a literary scholar and poet who has been published in many anthologies and given readings worldwide. Her best known volume of poetry is the award-winning *The African Saga* (1998).

**Okinba Launko** is the pen-name under which poet, critic, and playwright, Femi Osofisan, publishes his poetry. He is a well-known and prolific playwright, who recently retired from running the Department of Theatre Arts at Ibadan University in Nigeria.

**Rebecca Lim** recently completed her MA studies at the Division of English, Nanyang Technological University, Singapore. Her work in progress explores the power of storytelling in redeeming communities destabilized by different forms of social violence. Her work has appeared in the online *Singapore Review of Books*.

**Christina S. McMahon** is Assistant Professor of Theater at the University of California-Santa Barbara. She is the author of *Recasting Transnationalism through Performance: Theatre Festivals in Cape Verde, Mozambique, and Brazil* (2014). She is a past recipient of the IFTR New Scholar's Prize and a Fulbright-Hays grant. Her articles have appeared in *Theatre Research International, Theatre Survey, Theatre History Studies*, and the *Latin American Theatre Review*.

**Brendon Nicholls** teaches in African and Postcolonial Studies in the School of English, University of Leeds. He has published widely on Dambudzo Marechera, Nadine Gordimer, Bessie Head and Ngũgĩ wa Thiong'o. His major study on the work of Ngũgĩ is *Ngugi wa Thiong'o: Gender, and the Ethics of Postcolonial Reading* (2010).

**Chukwuma Okoye** is Head of the Department of Theatre Arts at the University of Ibadan in Nigeria. He has been a professional dancer and has wide-ranging research interests in Igbo performance forms, dance, film and contemporary theatre in Nigeria.

**Jane Plastow** is Professor of African Theatre and director of the Leeds University Centre for African Studies. She has worked directing, training, and researching in relation to theatre across East Africa for the past 30 years. Her most recent edited volume is *African Theatre Shakespeare: in and out of Africa* (2013).

**Mario Lúcio Sousa** was until recently Minister of Culture for Cape Verde and is now Ambassador of Culture. He is founder and leader of the musical group Simentera, and founder and director of the Quintal da Música Cultural Association. He has performed as a musician widely and internationally, and is also a painter, poet, novelist and playwright.

**Alemseged Tesfai** is a prominent Eritrean historian, essayist, novelist and playwright. He fought in the Eritrean Peoples Liberation Front from 1974-1990, and was the Head of Education and the Director of the Bureau of Cultural Affairs. His memoir of the liberation war, *Two Weeks in the Trenches* (2002), is published in both Tigrinya and English, and his most famous play, *The Other War,* has appeared in *Contemporary African Drama* (1999) and been performed across Eritrea, in the UK, and on BBC radio.

**Ngũgĩ wa Thiong'o** is a Kenyan playwright, novelist, and cultural commentator. He is currently Distinguished Professor of Comparative Literature at the University of California, Irvine. Key texts include the novels *A Grain of Wheat* (1967) and *Petals of Blood* (1977) and books of cultural commentary such as *Decolonising the Mind* (1986) and *Moving the Centre* (1994). Most recently he has been working on his memoirs with the second volume, *In the House of the Interpreter*, published in 2012.

---

# Moving Worlds
## Forthcoming issues include:

### Environment and Disaster (2014)
### Translating South East Asia (2015)

All titles subject to confirmation

---

# Stand

**'One of England's best, liveliest, and truly imaginative little magazines' - *Library Journal***

***Stand*** first appeared in 1952 when Jon Silkin used his redundancy pay to found a magazine to celebrate the role that art, poetry, and fiction could play in society.

Across its 60 year lifespan ***Stand*** has published poetry and prose writers including Geoffrey Hill, Tony Harrison, Helen Dunmore, Peter Carey, Angela Carter, Romesh Gunesekera, Jeffrey Wainwright, and others. Accepting unsolicited submissions by mail, the magazine continues to support new poetry, fiction, translation, and criticism.

'An outstanding quarterly... it has progressed to an international platform for avant-garde writers...' *Sunday Times*

'Earnest, urgent, elemental... describes the kind of English poetry it prints...' *Times Literary Supplement*

Ask for ***Stand*** at your local bookshop. Email engstand@leeds.ac.uk for more details or enquiries@worldwidesubscriptions.com for subscriptions. £6.50 per issue or £25 p/a.

**Send submissions (SAE included) to:**
The Editors, Stand Magazine, School of English, University of Leeds, Leeds, LS2 9JT.

**Website**: http://www.standmagazine.org
**Facebook**: Search for 'Stand Magazine'

# Mosaic

a journal for the interdisciplinary study of literature

# A matter of *lifedeath*

An international interdisciplinary conference

October 1-4, 2014

University of Manitoba
Winnipeg, Canada

Andrea Carlino
Françoise Dastur
David Palumbo-Liu
H. Peter Steeves
Elisabeth Weber

## Forthcoming Publications

**ROMANCE 47.2 (June 2014)** This *Mosaic* special issue engages the rich history of the word *Romance*, with essays on "the Romantics," the roman, romantic fiction, Romanticism, the state of the love story in literature and film, and the figure of the "romantic."

## Recent Publications

**FEATURING: NICHOLAS ROYLE 47.1 (March 2014)** Nicholas Royle is Professor of English at the University of Sussex. He is the author of numerous books, including *Veering* (2011) and the novel *Quilt* (2010). This issue will feature a "Crossings" interview with Professor Royle and new writing by him.

**BLINDNESS 46.3 (Sep. 2013)** This issue brings together critical and disability theories to address historical and contemporary studies and interpretations of blindness across various genres, as well as studies of, to use Samuel Weber's title words (in *Institution and Interpretation*), "The Blindness of the Seeing Eye."

*Mosaic, a journal for the interdisciplinary study of literature*
University of Manitoba
208 Tier Building
Winnipeg MB
R3T 2N2
Canada

Tel: 204-474-9763
Fax: 204-474-7584
mosaic@umanitoba.ca
www.umanitoba.ca/mosaic